MILET LANGUAGE LEARNING

Albany Public Library
Albany, NY

Starting
English

American English

TRACY TRAYNOR
ILLUSTRATED BY ANNA WILMAN

MILET

W9-CJD-124

Starting
English
American English

Milet Publishing
333 North Michigan Avenue
Suite 530
Chicago, IL 60601
info@milet.com
www.milet.com

Starting English
Written by Tracy Traynor
Illustrated by Anna Wilman

Adapted from British to American English by Eleise Jones

First published by Milet Publishing, LLC in 2006

Copyright © Tracy Traynor for text, 2006
Copyright © Milet Publishing, LLC, 2006

All rights reserved. No part of this publication may be reproduced in any
form or by any means without the written permission of the publishers.

You must not circulate this book in any other binding or cover and
you must impose this condition on any acquirer.

ISBN-13: 978 1 84059 492 8
ISBN-10: 1 84059 492 6

Printed and bound in China by Compass Press

Please see our website **www.milet.com** for more titles in the
Milet Language Learning series and for our range of bilingual books.

Contents

 # Introduction

Starting English is specially designed for people who already know some English and want to continue their learning in a stimulating and supportive way. It focuses on the language you need to cope with everyday situations (getting around, making arrangements, interacting with people, etc.). In particular, you will practice understanding spoken English and speaking English yourself. This course is ideal if you live in or want to visit an English-speaking country or do business with English speakers.

What is in the course

Starting English consists of a book and a CD. The book is in 12 units, with each unit in 3 sections. Each section focuses on a key objective (*Meeting people*, *Applying for a job*, etc.).

The book contains

- conversations to introduce and practice new language in a practical context
- grammar boxes to explain and give examples of language rules
- tips on culture and language, with particular focus on the U.S.
- activities at the end of the section to test your learning in context

- 3 *Review* sections, after Units 4, 8 and 12, to test you on the language you have just learned

The CD contains

- a recorded version of the main sentences and phrases for each section, with the opportunity to repeat them all
- a listening activity per unit, to test your understanding

How to use the course

- Read a conversation. First, try to understand it generally – don't worry about all the details. Try to summarize what it's about in your own language.
- Read it again. This time, try to understand the details. Use the grammar box to help you. Try to figure out any words you don't know. (Then, if necessary, look up words in a dictionary.)
- Write down any new words with a translation. Also keep a list of useful phrases.
- Read the grammar point and look for examples of it in the conversation.
- Read the tip box. Add any useful phrases here to your list.

- Then listen to the recording. You will see a prompt for this in the book:

  You can follow the text of the recording in the Transcript section on pp.89–92. Repeat each sentence after you hear it to improve your fluency and pronunciation. Play the recording as many times as you like.
- At the end of the section, do the *Try it out!* exercises to test yourself on what you've learned. (Some sections have a further exercise on the recording to test your understanding.)
- After Units 4, 8 and 12, do the Review section to test your progress.

Learning strategies

When to learn

You will learn most effectively if you study regularly. Doing a little English every day or a few times a week is better than one long session just once a week.

Set yourself objectives

To learn successfully, you need to decide what you want to achieve, e.g. *buy things in a shop* or *practice the present continuous tense*, etc. Make a short list before you start each session. At the end of your session, check through the list. Can you now do all the things?

It is important to keep reviewing vocabulary and structures from earlier units as you go along. Include this in your objectives.

Learning vocabulary

The *Wordlist* at the back of the book lists all the most important vocabulary in the course. It is designed so that you can write in translations in your own language. Use the *Wordlist* to test yourself: cover up one language and see if you can remember each word in the other language.

Coping with words you don't know

- Look at the context (the situation) – what is the word likely to mean?
- Does the word look like a word in your own language?
- Does the word look like another word in English that you know? (e.g. if you know *happy*, you can figure out *happiness*)
- Think about the grammar: is the word a noun, a verb, an adjective?

Further support

Starting English is designed so that you can use it to learn English on your own or in a class. If you are learning at home, it can help to learn **with a friend**. You can test each other and practice the conversations together – it can be more fun and easier to keep learning if you have someone else doing it with you.

Starting English has a Grammar section, summarizing all the grammar in the book. If you are interested, you might also want to buy a more detailed **grammar book**. This will give you more information on the grammar covered in *Starting English* and more examples. Some grammar books also contain exercises on particular grammar points, if you want further practice.

It is also a good idea to get and use a good **dictionary**. *Starting English* gives you the language you need to use in a wide range of practical situations; you can use your dictionary to expand your English with more details relevant to you.

What next?

- If you're learning on your own or with a friend, think about joining a language class to get more opportunity to practice.

- If you can, listen to English radio and watch English television. You can learn a lot from familiar program formats, such as the news, weather forecasts, and game shows. Check out English-language versions of your favorite websites. Read English newspapers and magazines to expand your vocabulary (these often have useful websites you can access too).

- Talk to English-speaking friends and colleagues as much as possible, and if you visit or live in an English-speaking country, use every opportunity to practice your English when you are out and about.

Meeting people

- Asking your name and giving my name
- Asking how you are and saying how I am
- Saying hello and goodbye

Hello. I'm Anna.

I'm Jake.

OR

What's your name?

My name's Jake.

She's Anna.

He's Jake.

Hi Jake, how are you?

I'm fine, thanks. And you?

I'm very well.

Grammar

The verb **to be** is usually shortened.

I**'m** = I **am**
he**'s** = he **is**
she**'s** = she **is**
you**'re** = you **are**

How are you?

I'm_____, thanks. And you?
- very well
- fine / OK

- not so good.
- terrible!

 **Now listen** to the recording for more practice.

Hello Hi

Hello Hi

Hello Hi

Good morning

Good afternoon

Good evening

Bye

Good night

See you soon

Goodbye

👁 Tip

You can say **Hello** or **Hi** at any time of day. **Hi** is quite informal.

Good morning, **Good afternoon,** and **Good evening** are all more formal. You will often hear them shortened (**Morning! Afternoon! Evening!**).

Use **Good night** only to say goodbye at the end of the evening. It is never used instead of **Hello**.

✋ Try it out!

- Greet someone and tell her your name.
- Ask what her name is.
- Ask how she is.
- Say how you are.

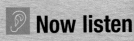 **Now listen**

My family

- Talking about my family
- Learning the numbers 1–10

Jake

Sally

Rosie

Mike

Emily

My mother, Rosie.
My father, Mike.
My sisters,
Emily and Sally.

I have three children —
one son and two daughters.

his children

He has three children.

I have one son and two daughters.

 her son

 her daughters

She has one son and two daughters.

I have one brother and one sister.

 her brother

 her sister

She has one brother and one sister.

Grammar

I **have**	one sister
he **has**	one daughter
she **has**	two sister**s**
	two daughter**s**

my brother
your sister
his/her mother
his/her father

Numbers

1 one

2 two

3 three

4 four

5 five

6 six

7 seven

8 eight

9 nine

10 ten

Grammar

one photo
ten photo**s**

but

one child
ten child**ren**

Tip

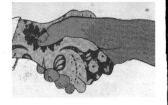

In the U.S., children generally call their parents **Mom** or **Mommy** and **Dad** or **Daddy**.

When families meet up after a long time apart, they will often kiss or hug. Men may instead shake hands with each other or pat each other on the back.

Try it out!

- How many . . .
  brothers
  sisters
  children
  . . . do you have?

- Draw your own family tree. Use it to talk about your family using **my**.

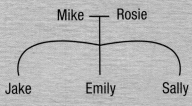

Mike ——— Rosie

Jake   Emily   Sally

Now listen

More about my family

- Saying more about my family
- Learning the numbers 11–20
- Giving my phone number and address

Daisy

Henry

Sarah

Ben

Joe

Tina

We're Jake's grandparents.
We're retired.

I'm Jake's cousin Ben.
I live on my own.

I'm Jake's cousin Tina.
I'm in school.

👄 Grammar

The verb **to be** is usually shortened.

we**'re** = we **are**
they**'re** = they **are**

| I **work** |
| he **works** |
| she **works** |

| Jake**'s** grandparents |

Jake

My aunt works
in a hospital.
She's a doctor.

My uncle works
in a store.
He sells computers.

 **Now listen**

Jake's my friend.

Anna's friend Jake.

Jake, what's your phone number?

It's 372-9481. What's yours?

Mine is 656-3329.

656-3329?

Yes, that's right.

I'll call you later.

Tip

Phone numbers are given in single numbers, with a slight pause between the sections: 5-5-4, 3-2-1-9. 0 (zero) is usually said as 'oh' in phone numbers. Sometimes, people will say the last four digits as two numbers instead of four single numbers: 3219 – 'thirty-two nineteen'.

To get help in an emergency (police, fire department, ambulance) call **911**. This number is free.

11 eleven

12 twelve

13 thirteen

14 fourteen

15 fifteen

16 sixteen

17 seventeen

18 eighteen

19 nineteen

20 twenty

What's your address?

My address is 523 Oak Street.

It's 1822 Linden Avenue.

Grammar

Jake**'s** my friend = Jake **is** my friend
Anna**'s** friend = the friend of Anna
it**'s** = it **is**

mine = **my** (phone number)
yours = **your** (phone number)
his = **his** (phone number)
hers = **her** (phone number)

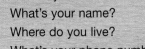 Try it out!

- Say your phone number and the phone numbers of your family.

- Give all your information.
  What's your name?
  Where do you live?
  What's your phone number?
  Now talk about your family.

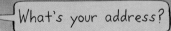 Listening task

- Write down the numbers.

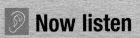 Now listen

Where I'm from

- Saying what country I'm from
- Giving my nationality and saying what language I speak
- Saying that something is correct or incorrect

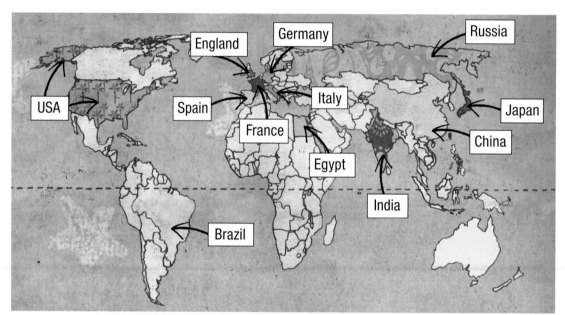

I'm from the United States.
I'm American.
Where are you from?

I'm from England.
I'm English.

This is Anna.
She's English.

This is Jake.
He's American.

 Grammar

I'm from **China**. I'm **Chinese**.
He's from **Italy**. He's **Italian**.

I'm French – I speak **French**.
I'm Japanese – I speak **Japanese**.
I'm Australian – I speak **English**.
I'm Egyptian – I speak **Arabic**.

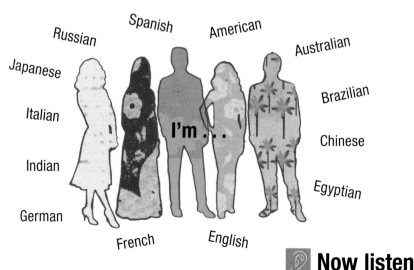

Russian
Spanish
American
Australian

Japanese
Brazilian

Italian
I'm . . .
Chinese

Indian
Egyptian

German
French
English

Now listen

Jake, this is my friend Cristina.

Hi, Cristina. Pleased to meet you.

Yes. I'm from Ohio. You're Spanish, aren't you?

It's a great party, isn't it?

Pleased to meet you too. You're American, is that right?

Yes, that's right. I'm from Granada in the south of Spain.

Yes, it is – very noisy!

Tip

When meeting people for the first time, it's usual to shake hands. When you're introduced, you say **Pleased to meet you** or **Nice to meet you**. In more formal contexts, you might also hear **How do you do?**

You'll often be asked about where you're from. Find your country/nationality in the dictionary, if it's not given here.

Grammar

Questions with a question word:

Where are you from?
Are you American too?
What's your name?

Questions with a tag:

You're Spanish, **aren't you?**
It's a great party, **isn't it?**

you**'re**...   ⟶   **aren't** you?
he**'s**...   ⟶   **isn't** he?
she**'s**...   ⟶   **isn't** she?
it**'s**...   ⟶   **isn't** it?

You can use **is that right?** instead of any of these tags.

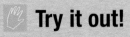

Try it out!

- Ask someone where he or she is from.
- Say where you're from.
- Give your nationality and say what languages you speak.
- Say that something is correct.

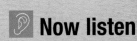

Now listen

More about me

- Answering questions about myself
- Talking more about my family
- Saying that something isn't the case

Do you live in New York?

Yes, I do.

No, I don't.

I live . . .

in the city

in the suburbs

in the country

on the coast

Are you married?

Yes, I am.

No, I'm not.

Grammar

Do you . . .

live in Brooklyn?
have any children?
work in Miami?

Yes, **I do.**
No, **I don't.**

Are you . . .

married?
here on your own?

Yes, **I am.**
No, **I'm not.**

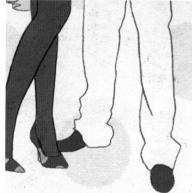

I'm . . .   **married**   **single**   **divorced**

 Now listen

Hi! I'm Sara. Pleased to meet you!

Hello! . . .

Yes, I'm married. My husband's name is Marco. He's Italian.

He works at the university.

No, we live near Chicago, in the suburbs.

We have two children, Katie and Paolo. They're in school. Katie's in grade school — she's in Fourth Grade. Paolo's in high school. He's in Ninth Grade.

Katie likes school, but Paolo doesn't like it.

Yes, I teach French at Paolo's school. School starts at nine and finishes at three.

Tip

In the U.S., children go to school when they're 5 years old. The first school is called **elementary school** (also called **grade school**). Many children go to **nursery** or **pre-school** before starting **kindergarten**. Classes after kindergarten are numbered: First Grade, Second Grade, etc. Children may go to **middle school** for Seventh and Eighth Grades, or they may go straight to **high school**, where they remain through Twelfth Grade.

Grammar

my husband**'s** name
my wife**'s** name
my children**'s** school

| he/she **likes** | he/she **doesn't like** |

Try it out!

- What did Jake say to Sara?
  What's your name? . . .
- Tell someone about Sara.
  Her husband works . . .
- Talk to Jake about your family.

 Now listen

What I do

- Saying what job I do
- Asking what you do
- Saying what I do if I don't work
- Talking about my job

I'm a journalist. What do you do?

I'm a teacher.

I'm a ...

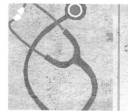

doctor   musician   teacher   receptionist   chef   bank teller

I work in a ...

hotel

hospital

school

restaurant

store

company

Grammar

Note that you use **a** with jobs.
I'm **a** teacher.

But if the word begins with a vowel (a, e, i, o, u) or a vowel sound (for example, **h**our) **a** becomes **an**:

I'm **an a**ccountant.

marketing

publishing

education

He's/She's in ...

finance

politics

banking

Now listen

Do you work?

I'm unemployed.

I'm a student.

I'm retired.

I'm still in school.

I look after my children.

Do you like your job?

Yes, I do.

I like it very much. It's really interesting!

It's not very interesting.

No, I don't. I don't like it at all!

It's OK.

👁 Tip

Talking about what you do is a really useful conversation topic. If it isn't covered here, find what you need in your dictionary, so you're ready with details of what you do (and where you work, if appropriate) and your opinion of it.

✋ Try it out!

- Tell Anna what you do and where you work. Say what you think of your job.

- Look up the words for the jobs your family and friends do, if they aren't given here. Can you say what each of them does?

  He's / She's a . . .

👂 Listening task

Listen and answer.

- Do they like their jobs?

  Yes, he / she does.
  No, he / she doesn't.

👄 Grammar

I **like**	I **don't like**
he/she **likes**	he/she **doesn't like**

It's really interesting.
It isn't very interesting.

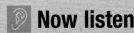 **Now listen**

Asking about places

- Saying what there is / isn't
- Saying where places are
- Asking what's near

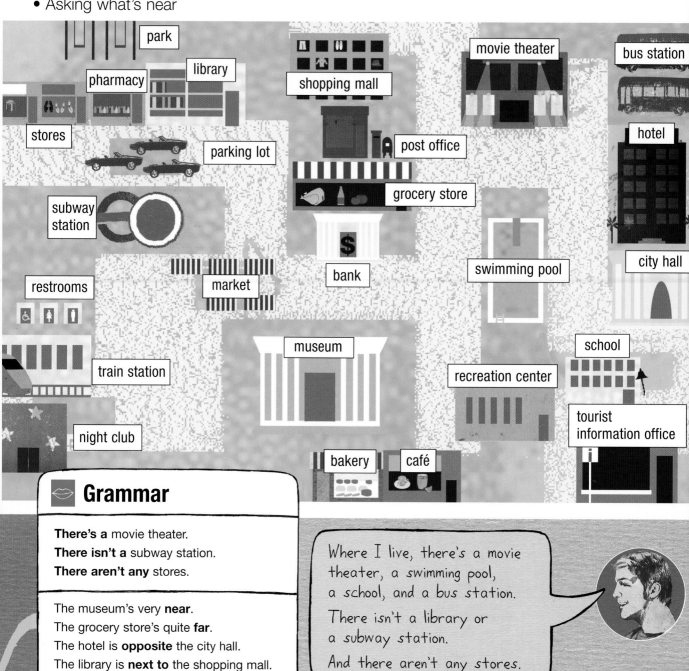

park
pharmacy
library
shopping mall
movie theater
bus station
stores
parking lot
post office
hotel
subway station
grocery store
restrooms
market
bank
swimming pool
city hall
train station
museum
recreation center
school
night club
tourist information office
bakery
café

Grammar

There's a movie theater.
There isn't a subway station.
There aren't any stores.

The museum's very **near**.
The grocery store's quite **far**.
The hotel is **opposite** the city hall.
The library is **next to** the shopping mall.
The post office is **between** the parking lot and the movie theater.

Where I live, there's a movie theater, a swimming pool, a school, and a bus station.

There isn't a library or a subway station.

And there aren't any stores.

Now listen

Excuse me. Is there a post office near here?

Yes, there is. There's one over there, next to the grocery store.

Thank you . . . Is there a bank near here?

A bank? Yes, there's a bank opposite the museum.

Where's the museum?

Go down here and turn right.

Is it far?

No, it's not far. About two minutes' walk.

And is there a pharmacy near here?

No, there isn't. There isn't a pharmacy near here.

Thanks for your help!

You're welcome.

Tip

When you're talking to someone you don't know – to ask for information or directions, for example – it's polite to begin by saying **Excuse me.** You can also add **Could you help me?** Don't be tempted to use **sir** or **ma'am** to address the person: these are used only in very formal situations. You don't need to call him/her anything.

Grammar

Is there a café near here?
Yes, **there is**.
No, **there isn't**.

Are there restrooms/stores near here?
Yes, **there are**.
No, **there aren't**.

 Try it out!

• Think about where you live. Tell Jake what's there and what isn't there. Use the pictures on p.18 for reference.

• You're visiting a new town. Ask someone about the following places:

 Is there a movie theater near here?

      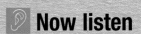 **Now listen**

Asking for directions

- Asking how to get somewhere
- Understanding directions
- Coping when I can't understand
- Thanking people and responding

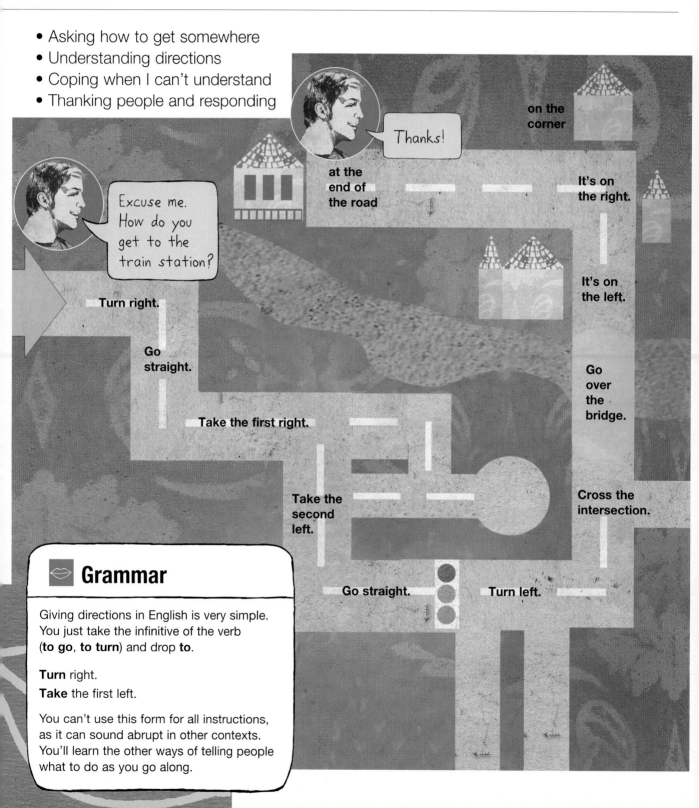

⬤ Grammar

Giving directions in English is very simple. You just take the infinitive of the verb (**to go**, **to turn**) and drop **to**.

Turn right.
Take the first left.

You can't use this form for all instructions, as it can sound abrupt in other contexts. You'll learn the other ways of telling people what to do as you go along.

Excuse me. How do you get to the Metro movie theater?

I'm sorry, I didn't catch that. Could you say it again, please?

Thank you.

Is it far?

Thank you very much.

The Metro . . . Go along this road to the stoplight. Cross the road and turn left.

Of course. Along this road as far as the stoplight. Cross then turn left.

Then take the third right. The Metro is at the end of the street on the left.

It's not far — about five minutes' walk.

No problem!

👁 Tip

If you're finding it difficult to understand what people say, the following expressions can help you:

I'm sorry, I didn't catch that. Could you say it again? Could you speak more slowly, please?

To thank someone:
thank you
thank you very much

and less formally:
thanks
many thanks

In response you will hear:
You're welcome.
Don't mention it.
No problem! (informal)

👄 Grammar

Ways of saying how far away something is:

five minutes' walk
ten minutes by car
twenty minutes on the bus

✋ Try it out!

• Use the map on p.20 to practice giving directions. Start from the pink arrow.

• Give directions to a friend from her house to your house.

👂 Listening task

• Repeat the directions.

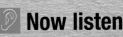

👂 Now listen

How I travel

- Saying how I travel
- Learning the numbers 21–100+
- Asking for travel information

I go by . . .

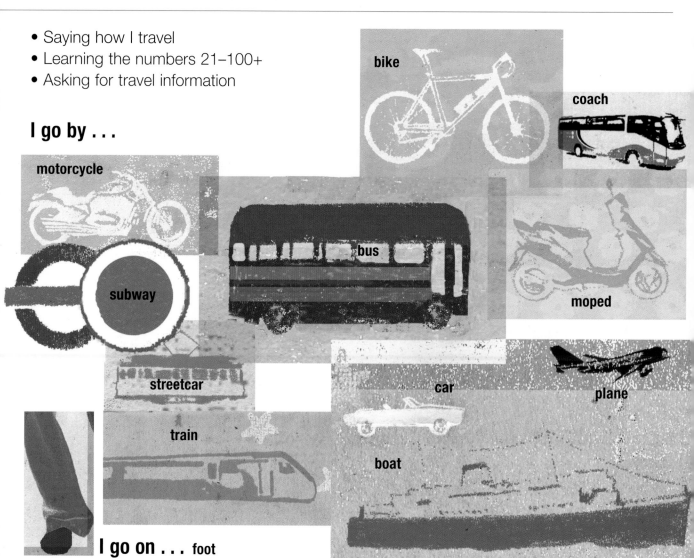

bike

coach

motorcycle

bus

moped

subway

streetcar

car

plane

train

boat

I go on . . . foot

Grammar

by bike, bus, train, etc.
but
on foot

Numbers 21–100+

20	twenty	21	twenty-one	76	seventy-six
30	thirty	32	thirty-two	87	eighty-seven
40	forty	43	forty-three	98	ninety-eight
50	fifty	54	fifty-four	109	one hundred and nine
60	sixty	65	sixty-five		
70	seventy				
80	eighty				
90	ninety				
100	one hundred				

Now listen

Try it out!

- Tell Anna how you travel to school/work/the store/the library, etc. Try to use the words you know to make sentences.

  I go to school by bus.

- Get to know English numbers by practicing them every day. Whenever you see a number (a bus number, a page number, a telephone number), say the English for it. This will really help you remember them.

Grammar

Which bus goes to the Science Museum?

need is followed by the infinitive:
You **can take** the number 43.
but
You **need to catch** the number 51.

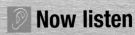
Now listen

Buying food

- Shopping for food
- Learning bigger numbers
- Expressing quantities
- Asking if items are available

> I'd like some apples, please.

> I'd like a box of chocolates, please.

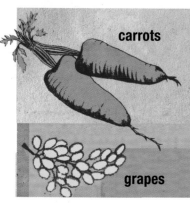

carrots

grapes

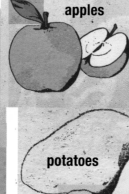

apples

strawberries

tomatoes

peppers

potatoes

chicken

fish

apple juice

rice

orange juice

bottled water

cookies

cake

chips

chocolates

Grammar

You can use **some** with all of the food items shown or use the following quantities/containers:

a pound of apples
half a pound/8 ounces of grapes
a quarter of a pound/4 ounces of cheese

a box of cookies/crackers
a bag of chips/candy
a bar of chocolate
a pint of strawberries

a carton of fruit juice/milk
a bottle of water

a cake
a chicken

149	one hundred and forty-nine
200	two hundred
350	three hundred and fifty
490	four hundred and ninety
1000	a thousand
1425	one thousand four hundred and twenty-five

Now listen

Good morning. What would you like?

Yes — good grapes. Very sweet.

8 oz. of grapes . . . here you are.

How many would you like?

Anything else?

How much would you like?

Is that everything?

Grapes, apples, cheese, strawberries . . . that's $11.75 (eleven dollars and seventy-five cents).

Twenty dollars — that's 8.25 (eight twenty-five) change.

Do you have any grapes?

I'll have half a pound.

And some apples, please.

I'll have four of those.

Yes — some cheese, please.

4 oz. . . . And a pint of strawberries.

Yes, that's everything, thanks.

Thank you.

Thanks. Bye.

Tip

The currency in the U.S. is the **dollar**. 100 pennies make $1 (one penny is also called one **cent**; change under one dollar is referred to as **cents**). When you say prices consisting of dollars and cents, the words **dollar(s)** and **cent(s)** are often left out: $1.50 – **one dollar and fifty cents** or **one fifty**.

Grammar

In English, some nouns are called uncountable: water, juice, cheese, rice, pasta, cereal, etc.

This means they are never used as plurals or with **a/an** or numbers. Compare this with the countable noun **apple**: **two** apple**s**, **an** apple.

With uncountable nouns, you use **How much . . . ?** With countable nouns, you use **How many . . . ?**

How **much** cheese would you like?
How **many** apples would you like?

some, **any** and **a lot of** can be used with countable and uncountable nouns:

I'd like **some** cheese/apples.
Do you have **any** cheese/apples?
She buys **a lot of** cheese/apples.

> **I'd** like = I **would** like
> **I'll** have = I **will** have

Try it out!

• You're in a grocery store. Tell the clerk you want to find the following things: bananas, tomatoes, pizza, bottled water, apple juice and chips. Make up the quantities. Remember to include hello, please, thank you, and goodbye in your conversation.

• Look in your kitchen. Can you name all the foods you find there in English? Include quantities/containers.

Listening task

• What does Jake buy? How much is it?

 Now listen

Buying clothes

- Learning the words for clothes
- Learning how to describe clothes
- Talking about sizes
- Getting help in a store

white gym shoes

brown shoes

black boots

a white T-shirt

orange shorts

a pink skirt

a blue jacket

a red tie

blue jeans

green pants

black tights

a grey shirt

a purple dress

a green sweatshirt

a pink sweater

a red hat

a brown belt

an orange coat

blue socks

purple sandals

a yellow baseball cap

👄 Grammar

Colors are adjectives. Adjectives tell you more about a noun.

In English, adjectives are the same for singular items and plural items.

a **red** coat – it's **red**

blue jeans – they're **blue**

(Note that **jeans**, **pants**, **shorts**, **tights** are all plural in English. So you buy **some** jeans, or **a pair of** jeans, not **a** jeans.)

small

too small

very small

big

too big

very big

 **Now listen**

Try it out!

- You're in a store. Ask for help – you want to try on some pants, a T-shirt and boots. Work out your sizes and pick the colors, then imagine your conversation with the assistant.

- Look at a magazine. What clothes are people wearing? Describe them.

Tip

As well as numbered sizes for clothes, some shops use the following labels:

S – small, M – medium, L – large, XL – extra large.

Find out your clothes size and shoe size and have the information ready when you go shopping.

Now listen

Buying presents

- Describing what I want
- Comparing things
- Making myself understood when I don't know the word

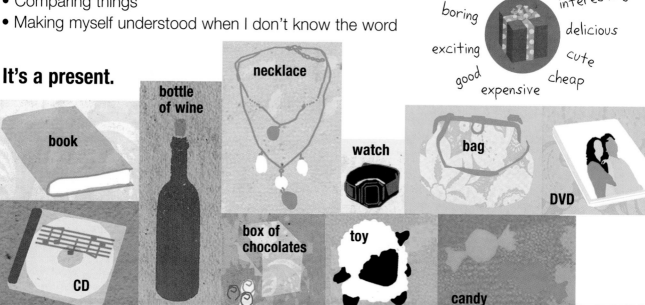

pretty   useful
boring   interesting
exciting   delicious
good   cute
expensive   cheap

It's a present.

necklace

bottle of wine

book

watch

bag

DVD

CD

box of chocolates

toy

candy

 Grammar

The comparative is used to compare two things.

Short adjectives add -**er**:
(note **y ➞ i**)

cheap   cheap**er**
pret**ty**   pret**tier**

Long adjectives use **more**:

expensive   **more** expensive

A toy is **cuter than** a bag.
A watch is **more useful than** a necklace.

good and **bad** have irregular comparatives:
This book is **good**, but that book is **better**.
The green hat is **bad** but the blue is **worse**!

I'm looking for a present for Emily.

What does she like?

She likes books and CDs. Is this book good?

Not really — it's boring. What about a necklace? Look at those . . .

 **Now listen**

I'm looking for a necklace for my sister.

These green necklaces are pretty.

Maybe the blue ones are prettier than the green. How much are they?

Those necklaces are $45.

That's too expensive. Do you have anything cheaper?

This pink one is $30 — or we have this purple necklace at $35.

The purple one is better, I think. I'll take that one.

How are you paying?

By credit card.

Could you sign here, please?

And here's your receipt. Thank you very much.

Tip

If an American friend invites you to dinner at his/her home, it is usual to take a small present, like a bottle of wine, a box of chocolates, or flowers. A typical gift from your own country would be even better. If there are children in the house, a book or a small toy is also a good idea.

Grammar

To talk about something near, use **this** and **these**.

Is **this** book good?
How much are **these**?

To talk about something farther away, use **that** and **those**.

Can I see **that** toy, please?
Can I try **those** jeans in pink, please?

You can use **this/that (one)** or **these/those (ones)** on their own, if it's clear what you mean – this is very useful if you don't know the word for something.

Can I try **this** in a size 10, please?
What about **these**?
I think **that one** looks good on you.
Those ones are too expensive.

Try it out!

• Look at all the pictures of presents on p.28. Ask how much they cost, using **this** or **these** as appropriate.

• Now describe the items in the pictures. Pick an adjective for each.

an interesting DVD

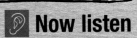 Now listen

Review 1

1 Add the verb

1 I _have_ two brothers.

2 My name _____ Anna.

3 I _____ it very much.

4 We _____ Jake's parents.

5 Where _____ you from?

6 She _____ English.

7 This _____ my friend Amir.

8 He _____ in a hospital.

9 I _____ a photographer.

10 _____ a grocery store near here?

2 Find the food

1 neckchi   _chicken_

2 sicekoo   _____

3 tamesoot   _____

4 bareswetirrs   _____

5 gareno eciju   _____

6 gab fo dnayc   _____

7 xbo fo hotscolace   _____

8 lebtot fo newi   _____

9 pduon fo peasgr   _____

10 noctra fo klim   _____

3 Write the nationality and the language

1 I'm from Spain   _I'm Spanish. I speak Spanish._

2 I'm from China.

3 I'm from Russia.

4 I'm from the United States.

5 I'm from Brazil.

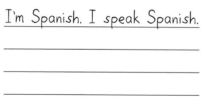

4 Answer the questions

1 What's your name?

2 How are you?

3 What's your phone number?

4 What's your address?

5 Where are you from?

6 Are you American?

7 Are you married?

8 Do you live in the country?

9 What do you do?

10 Do you like your job?

5 Put the words in the right order

1 pharmacy here a near there is?   _Is there a pharmacy near here?_

2 bus get do to how you station the?   _____

3 to this along stoplight road the go.   _____

4 take right second the then.   _____

5 right Museum the for the is Science this bus?   _____

6 please grapes some like I'd.   _____

7 like much very I it.   _____

8 have 8 a size you in do them?   _____

9 them in try please I orange can   _____

10 one this that is than interesting CD more.   _____

6 Buying a present

Answer the sales assistant using the words given.
Look back at Unit 4 if you need help.

• Can I help you?

— looking / present / brother   _I'm looking for a present for my brother._

• What does he like?

— CDs / DVDs _____

• What about this DVD? It's very exciting.

— not / his / thing _____

— that / one? _____

— good? _____

• That one is even better. It's more exciting.

— how / much? _____

• This one costs $19.99.

— too / expensive _____

— cheaper? _____

• This DVD is cheaper and it's more interesting than the first one.

— take / it _____

— thanks _____

Getting information

- Learning the days of the week
- Getting information about a class
- Saying when I do things
- Talking on the telephone

> I work from Monday to Friday, but in the evenings and on the weekend, I have free time.

MONDAY

On Mondays
I go to the gym.

TUESDAY

On Tuesdays
I do the grocery
shopping.

WEDNESDAY

On Wednesdays
I watch television.

THURSDAY

On Thursdays
I don't do anything.

FRIDAY

On Fridays
I see my friends.

SATURDAY

On Saturdays
I go to the movies.

SUNDAY

On Sundays
I relax. I read
the paper, drink
coffee, and listen
to the radio.

 Grammar

On Mondays I go to the gym.
from Monday **to** Friday

Present tense: The tense used here is the **present simple**: this is the verb form that you have been using so far. It is used for things that happen *regularly*.

On Mondays I **go** to the gym.

Now listen

Hello? Is this Norton College?

Yes, it is.

I'm calling about the language classes.

Are you looking for a French course? I'm afraid they're all full.

No, I'm interested in Spanish.

What level are you?

Beginner, I think. I know a little Spanish, but not much.

Beginner . . . yes, there are places in the beginner Spanish class. That's on Tuesdays.

When does it start?

On Tuesday the 20th of September. It starts at seven o'clock and finishes at eight.

How much does it cost?

It's $40 a term. You can send us a check or pay on the night.

That sounds great. Thank you.

👁 Tip

When you answer the phone, all you have to say is **Hello**.

When you're calling someone, to confirm you've got the right person, you can say **Hello, is this . . . ?**

👄 Grammar

English has a second present tense, the **present continuous**. It is used for things that are happening *right now*.

I'm calling about the language classes.

Are you **looking** for a French course?

See p.40 for how this tense is formed.

What time is it?

It's three o'clock.
It's four o'clock.

It starts **at** six o'clock and finishes **at** nine.

Note that sometimes the word **o'clock** is dropped.

✍ Try it out!

• Say what Jake does every day. Use the pictures in his agenda, but don't look at the sentences!

On Mondays, I go to the gym.

• What time is it?

3:00	It's 3 o'clock
4:00	6:00
7:00	1:00
10:00	8:00
12:00	9:00

 Now listen

Signing up

- Learning dates
- Talking about time
- Asking for information
- Signing up

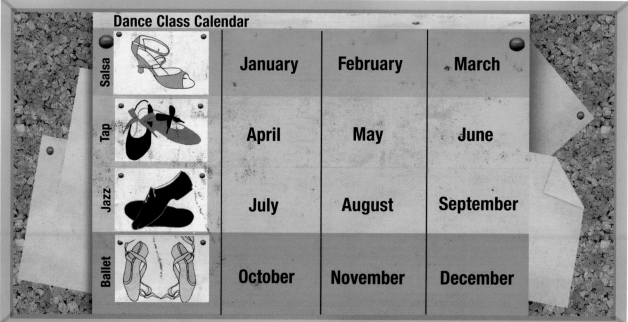

Dance Class Calendar

Salsa	January	February	March
Tap	April	May	June
Jazz	July	August	September
Ballet	October	November	December

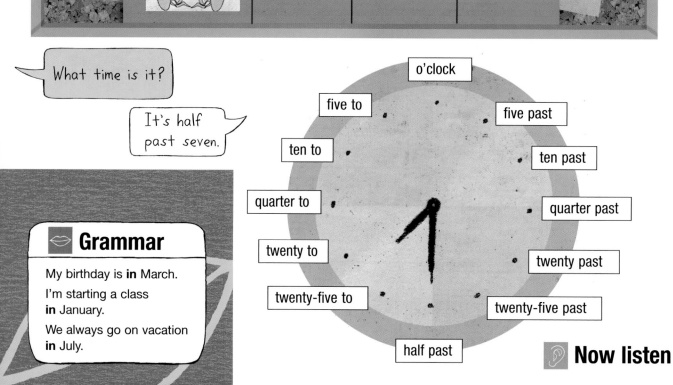

What time is it?

It's half past seven.

o'clock
five to
five past
ten to
ten past
quarter to
quarter past
twenty to
twenty past
twenty-five to
twenty-five past
half past

👄 Grammar

My birthday is **in** March.

I'm starting a class **in** January.

We always go on vacation **in** July.

👂 **Now listen**

Hello —
Active Dance.

Hello, I'm calling about your salsa dance class.

Oh, yes. How can I help you?

When is it?

The class is on Friday nights. The next class starts in January . . . Let's see . . . It starts on the 14th of January.

At what time?

Seven-thirty until nine.

Are there spaces still available?

Yes, there are. But it's quite popular — if you're interested, you should sign up soon.

I'm a complete beginner — does that matter?

It doesn't matter at all! We teach all levels.

Can I sign up, please?

Of course. Can you hang on a minute? I'll just get a pen and take your information . . .

👄 Grammar

Dates in English use ordinal numbers: 1st, 2nd, 3rd, etc.

My birthday is **on** the first **of** May.

1st	first
2nd	second
3rd	third
4th	fourth
5th	fifth

Then you just add **th** to the each number (**six**th), with the following exceptions (these mainly affect spelling not pronunciation!).

8th	eighth
9th	ninth
12th	twelfth
20th	twentieth
21st	twenty-first, etc.
30th	thirtieth
31st	thirty-first

✋ Try it out!

- Practice dates. Give the birthdays of your family and friends.

My mother's / Her birthday is on the fifth of June.

- You want to join a dance class. You need to find out all about it. Think what questions you need to ask.

 Now listen

Giving information

- Spelling my name
- Giving information
- Confirming arrangements

Alphabet:

A B C D E F
G H I J K L
M N O P Q R
S T U V W X
Y Z

How do you spell your last name? Is it Miller with an E?

No, with an A for apple. M — I — L — L — A — R.

 Tip

Some letters in English sound similar to each other. If you want to be completely clear, copy Anna and use a word: *a for apple*. It doesn't really matter what words you use as long as they're clear.

In the U.S., people are asked for their first and last names. They put their given name (**Anna**) first, and their family name **Millar** last: **Anna Millar**.

Many given names have short forms (e.g. **Jim** for **James**, **Tom** for **Thomas**), used by friends and family. If someone says his name is Jim, then call him that, but if he introduces himself as **James**, don't call him **Jim** unless he invites you to do so.

 **Now listen**

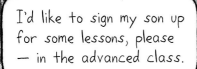

I'd like to sign my son up for some lessons, please — in the advanced class.

Has he been here before?

No, he hasn't.

OK — I just need to take some information . . . What's your son's name?

Paolo Vincente.

How do you spell that?

Paolo — that's P — A — O — L — O and Vincente — that's V — I — N — C — E — N — T — E.

Thank you. How old is he?

He's thirteen.

Great. Could you write your telephone number here, please, and sign the form?

That's $45, please.

Thanks.

So, the course starts on Friday the 22nd at 4:30 [four-thirty] and it runs for eight weeks?

That's right.

👁 Tip

You will often hear times given in the following way:

5:20	five-twenty
6:30	six-thirty
8:55	eight fifty-five

In the U.S., the 24-hour clock is not often used. Times are stated as **am** for morning and **pm** for afternoon and evening. Midnight is 12:00am, and noon is 12:00pm.

🖐 Try it out!

- Spell your name and the names of all the people in your family.
- Confirm these arrangements:
  swimming lessons / beginners / October 3 / 5:00–6:00

👂 Listening task

- Listen and write down the answers.

  What is the class?
  When is it?
  When does it start?
  How much does it cost?

👄 Grammar

Has he/she **been** here before?
No, he/she **hasn't**.

  **Now listen**

Traveling by train

- Asking about train times
- Asking for other travel details
- Buying a ticket

I need to get to the city by 9:30.

Do you have a schedule?

OR

Is there a train that leaves about 8?

OR

When is the next train?

There's a train at 8:02, which arrives at 9:15. Or the 8:25, arriving at 9:25.

OR

The next train is the 8:25.

How long does it take?

It takes about an hour.

When does it arrive?

It arrives at 9:25.

Do I have to change?

Yes — you have to change at St. James.

OR

No, it's direct.

👄 Grammar

Questions with question words

How long does it take?

When does it leave/arrive?

When are you coming back?

Which platform does it leave from?

Other questions

Is this the Denver train?

Is this ticket valid?

Yes, it **is**.

No, it **isn't**.

Is there . . . ?

There's . . . = There is . . .

 Tip

In some cities, there are various types of train tickets available depending on what time of day you want to travel. If you can travel **off peak** – between around 9:00am and 4:00pm or after 6:30pm – tickets are usually much cheaper.

All travel distances are in miles
(1 km = about $5/8$ mile).

Sometimes announcements are used to give up-to-date information in a train station. They aren't always very clear, so concentrate on listening for key words:

The 7:04 to Wichita is running approximately 10 minutes **late**.

The 12:18 to Boston is **delayed**.

This service has been **cancelled**.

The 5:10 Express will **depart** from **Platform 4**.

Try it out!

- Review times with a bus or train schedule. Practice reading them aloud in English.

- You want to go to Boston. You need to be there by 12:30 and leave at around 7:30 in the evening. Plan what you would ask at the train station.

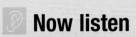 **Now listen**

At the airport

- Saying what I'm going to do
- Checking in at the airport

👄 Grammar

The **present continuous** is used to say what's happening right now (**I'm looking** for the check-in desk – see Unit 5, p.33).

It is also used to talk about the future:

I'm meeting him there.
He**'s flying** direct to Boston.
On Monday, she**'s going** to the gym.

I'm
you're
he's/she's
we're
you're
they're

} + verb+ing

I'm going
we're meeting
they're coming

Speech bubbles:

Hi, Anna? Where are you going?

On your own?

That sounds great. I'm here to pick up Kim. Her flight is landing in five minutes.

We're meeting some friends for a drink tonight. Tomorrow I'm playing football, then we're going to a movie.

When is your flight?

You too!

I'm going to Boston for the weekend!

No, with Dan. He's in Detroit — he's flying direct to Boston and I'm meeting him there. We're staying with friends.

What are you doing this weekend?

Sounds good.

It leaves in an hour — I better check in now. Have a good weekend!

👂 **Now listen**

Try it out!

- Write a list of things that you/your family are going to do on the weekend. Use a dictionary if you need to.

I'm going to a movie with my boyfriend/girlfriend.

- Now imagine you can do anything you want to this weekend and write another list. Try to use the vocabulary you have learned so far as much as possible.

I'm flying to New Orleans. I'm going to Mardi Gras.

Tip

The following phrases are useful for finding out about ongoing travel:

Excuse me . . .

Is there a bus/train to the center of town?

Where is the bus stop/train station/subway station?

Do you have a schedule?

How much is the taxi fare to . . . ?

Now listen

Making a reservation

- Reserving a room in a hotel
- Reserving a table in a restaurant

Tip

Some useful phrases if you're traveling and booking accommodation as you go:

Do you have a single / double room free for tonight / two nights?

Do you have a room for four people / a suite with a kitchen?

Is breakfast included?

Is there a swimming pool?

What time is check-out?

Is there a charge for parking?

Like phone numbers, credit card numbers are given in single figures.

I'd like to reserve a room, please.

Yes, of course. For when?

From the 9th of November to the 12th.

The 9th to the 12th . . . for 3 nights. Single or double?

A double room, please.

Yes, we have a double room available.

How much is it?

$105 a night.

Is breakfast included?

Yes, it is.

I'll take it. My name is Jake Ravens.

Could I take your credit card number, Mr. Ravens?

Yes, of course. It's 6544 . . .

Thank you, Mr. Ravens. We look forward to seeing you on the 9th.

Now listen

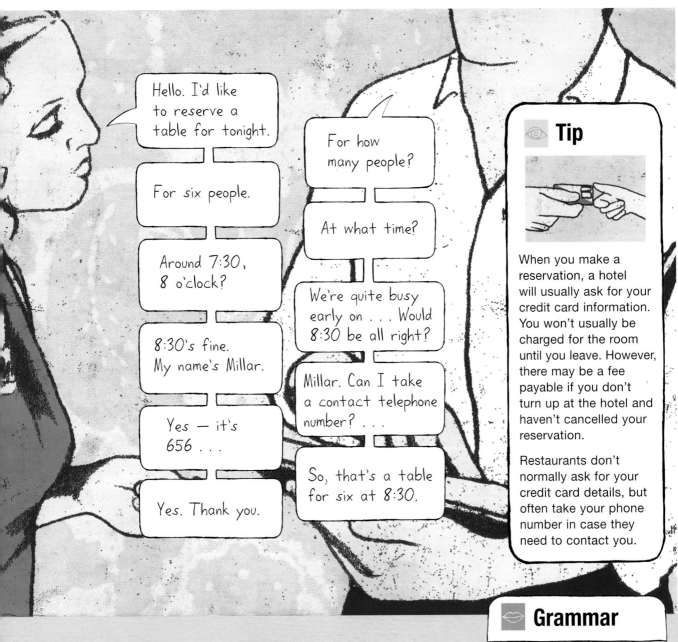

Tip

When you make a reservation, a hotel will usually ask for your credit card information. You won't usually be charged for the room until you leave. However, there may be a fee payable if you don't turn up at the hotel and haven't cancelled your reservation.

Restaurants don't normally ask for your credit card details, but often take your phone number in case they need to contact you.

Grammar

For **how many** nights?
For **how many** people?
I'd like to reserve a table **for tonight**.
I'd like to reserve a table **for Saturday**.

$105 **a night**.
$40 **a term**.

Try it out!

- Reserve a table:
  For 7 / at 9:30 / on Friday

  I'd like to reserve a table for seven at nine-thirty on Friday.

  For 4 / 8:15 / Sat
  For 5 / 6:30 / Wed, July 24
  For 2 / 8:00 / Thurs, Dec 21

Listening task

- Listen and note down the details.

  What kind of room does Anna want?

  When does she want it and for how long?

  How much does it cost?

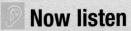 **Now listen**

Visiting a friend

- Giving/accepting/refusing an invitation
- Making/accepting/refusing an offer
- Learning some snacks and drinks

👁 Tip

The expression **Please help yourself/yourselves** is very useful (**yourself** when you are talking to one person, **yourselves** when it's more than one). Not only does it mean you don't have to remember all the words for the things you're offering – it's also very friendly!

👄 Grammar

Would you like . . .	a cookie? a cheese sandwich? some milk? some more cake? another sandwich? some more?
Could I have . . .	tea, please? a cup of coffee, please? some sugar, please? a glass of water, please?

Would you like to come over for coffee?

Thanks — I'd love to!

I'm sorry, I can't.

I'll have coffee, please.

Would you like tea or coffee?

Could I have tea, please?

Please help yourselves to cookies.

No, thanks. I'm fine.

Would you like some more cake?

Yes, please . . . It's delicious!

Some more coffee, Tess?

Thank you.

👂 **Now listen**

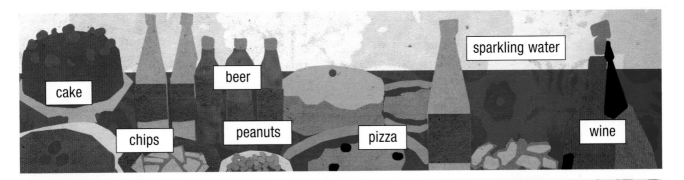

Grammar

What would you like . . .	to eat? to drink?
Can I get you . . .	something to eat? something to drink?
Would you like . . .	a glass of red wine? a glass of sparkling water? a beer? a slice of pizza? some water? some peanuts? some chips?
	To review countable and uncountable nouns in English, see p.25.

Try it out!

- Imagine you're having friends over to your house for coffee. Figure out how you would welcome them and what you would offer them to drink and to eat.

- Practice countable and uncountable nouns next time you are at the grocery store. Or use the food in your kitchen!

Listening task

- What does the man have to eat and drink?

- What does the woman have?

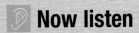 **Now listen**

Ordering in a café

- Saying how I'm feeling
- Making a suggestion
- Ordering a drink/snack

I'm hungry.   **I'm thirsty.**   **I'm cold.**   **I'm hot.**   **I'm tired.**

Do you want to have a cup of coffee?

Should we go to this café?

Good idea. I'm really thirsty!

That would be great!

👄 Grammar

I'm starving! = I'm **very**/**really** hungry!
I'm parched! = I'm **very**/**really** thirsty!
I'm exhausted! = I'm **very**/**really** tired!
I'm freezing! = I'm **very**/**really** cold!
I'm boiling! = I'm **very**/**really** warm!

To talk about how other people feel, revise the verb **to be**:

I'm	we're
you're	you're
he's/she's/it's	they're

👂 Now listen

Could we see a menu, please?

Of course.

What are you having?

I'm a little hungry . . . I think I'll have coffee and a sandwich. A chicken sandwich. What about you?

I can't decide. I don't think I feel like a snack.

What about some cake?

Yes, that sounds good.

Are you ready to order?

Yes, I think so. A cappuccino and a salmon bagel, please.

I'll have an espresso and . . . a piece of chocolate cake. Thank you.

I thought you said a chicken sandwich?

I changed my mind!

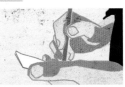

👁 Tip

In English, people say **please** and **thank you** a lot! It's considered rude to say just **yes** or **no**. **Please** is used whenever you ask for something and **thank you** whenever someone gives you something or does something for you.

To get a waiter's attention when you are eating out, say **Excuse me**. Gesturing or making a sound to make him/her notice you is also considered rude.

👄 Grammar

You use **What would you like?** if you are offering something that is yours or that you will pay for. In a situation like a restaurant, where you're going to share the cost, use **What are you having?**

I think and **I don't think** are often used when you haven't completely made up your mind about something.

I think I'll have a sandwich.

I don't think I feel like a snack.

Yes, **I think** so. Here **I think so** is used because **Yes** on its own sounds abrupt.

✋ Try it out!

• Practice the verb **to be**. Say how you and all the members of your family feel.

He's really tired.

• Practice ordering in a café. Order for your friends too.

– Ask for the menu.

– You'll have coffee and a cheese sandwich.

– Your friends will have wine and pizza/tea and pasta salad.

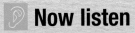 **Now listen**

Ordering in a restaurant

- Reading a menu
- Asking what things are
- Ordering a meal

Menu

Appetizers

Soup tomato soup, clam chowder

Salad mixed salad, Greek salad

Smoked salmon, mussels, asparagus

Specials

Beef in Burgundy with porcini mushrooms $10.95

Swordfish with herb crust, saffron rice $11.95

Strawberry pavlova $4.95

Main course

Meat roast chicken, ribeye steak, lasagna

Fish tuna, sea bass

Vegetarian red pepper tart, mushroom risotto

Choose from baked potato, french fries, salad, mixed vegetables

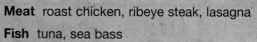

Dessert

Cakes cheesecake, chocolate cake

Ice cream vanilla, strawberry

Fruit raspberries, pineapple, fruit salad

Wine

House red

Isla Negar – Chilean Cabernet Sauvignon

$3.25/glass
$12.95/bottle

Tip

In addition to the menu, many restaurants also have a short list of dishes being cooked specially that day. These are called specials and are shown on a board or on an additional page in the menu.

Restaurants often have a recommended wine called the house wine, which is usually good value. Ask for a bottle/ a glass of the house red/white. Alternatively, you can choose from the wine list.

I reserved a table for 8:30. The name's Millar.

Yes, a table for 2. This way, please.

Tip

The U.S. has a strong tradition of regional food. For example: in New England, clam chowder; in the Deep South, key lime pie; on the West Coast, sourdough bread; and in the Midwest, corn on the cob.

When you eat out you'll also come across food from many different countries, so it can be difficult to know what everything on the menu is. Learn the vocabulary for ingredients (onions, apples, etc.) and go prepared to ask:

What's . . . ?
What are . . . ?
or **What's in ... ?**

If you have any special requirements in your diet, it's a good idea also to be ready to explain them.

Does it contain nuts/meat/onions/eggs?

I can't eat nuts/meat/onions/eggs.

Try it out!

• Look at the menu on p.48. Using the categories (soup, meat, etc.), can you guess what each thing is? Check your answers in the dictionary.

• Keep an eating out list – write down all the different dishes you try or find out about and what they are. (Add the contact details of your favorite restaurants too!)

In my free time

- Talking about my free time activities
- Saying when and how often I do things

What do you do in your free time?

I go . . .

out with friends

for a bike ride

to the movies

I play . . .

the piano

the drums

the guitar

I go . . .

swimming

dancing

shopping

I play . . .

tennis

soccer

badminton

Now listen

I play tennis once a week.

I go to the movies every Wednesday.

I eat out whenever I can!

 Tip

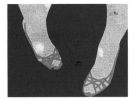

People often ask about your hobbies and interests (what you do in your free time), so be prepared. Use a dictionary to find out the words for any activities you don't know and be ready to say how often you do them and to give your opinion on them too (*I love dancing! I enjoy it very much.*)

On the weekend I see my family. They come for dinner.

I go swimming twice a week.

In the evening I watch television or read a book.

On Sunday mornings I sleep late.

I have guitar lessons three times a week.

I go to a class on Thursdays — I'm learning to cook.

 Grammar

When do you . . . ?

on Mondays

on Tuesday mornings

in the morning / afternoon / evening

on the weekend

whenever I can

How often do you . . . ?

once / twice / three times a week

every Saturday

Try it out!

- Make a list of the activities your family does. How often do they do each one? What do they think of them? Add as much detail as you can.

My brother plays soccer at school. He plays twice a week, but he doesn't really like it.

Talking about what I like

- Saying what I like/don't like watching on television
- Talking about what's on

> What do you like watching on television?

music programs

dramas

comedies

documentaries

movies

> I like . . .

the news

the weather forecast

soaps

> I don't mind . . .

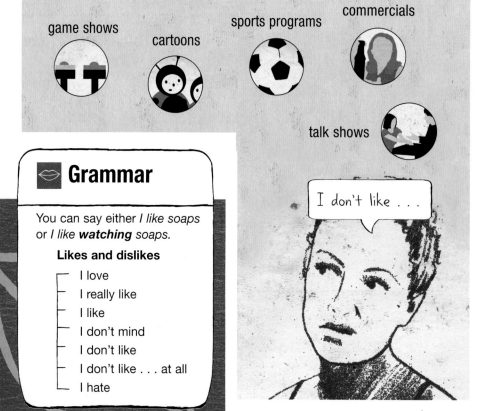

game shows

cartoons

sports programs

commercials

talk shows

> I don't like . . .

👄 Grammar

You can say either *I like soaps* or *I like **watching** soaps.*

Likes and dislikes

- I love
- I really like
- I like
- I don't mind
- I don't like
- I don't like . . . at all
- I hate

👁 Tip

Television is not only a good topic of conversation, it's also a great way to practice your English. Start with programs which have a familiar format – soaps, game shows, commercials, the weather forecast. You know the kind of language that is going to be used and this will help you figure out words you don't know.

👂 Now listen

Try it out!

- Look at the television listings in a newspaper or magazine. Can you say in English what's on tonight and when? Do you like watching these programs?

- Pick your three favorite programs. How often do you watch them?

Listening task

- What's on and when?
- What programs do the man and the woman like?

Grammar

How often do you watch . . . ?
always
sometimes
never

Opinions	interesting
	boring
	exciting
It's/	moving
They're . . .	funny
	sad
	informative
	entertaining

kind of and **really** can be useful terms if you want to be less direct about your opinions (the people here know each other well!).
I prefer . . . is also a polite way of expressing an opinion.

I don't **really** like . . .
I find it **kind of** boring . . .
I prefer . . .

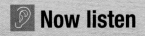 **Now listen**

What I like doing

- Talking about the weather
- Saying what I like doing
- Saying what I will or won't do, depending on the weather

When it's sunny, we like going for a walk in the country.

I go shopping in any weather!

When it's snowing, I like staying in and reading books and magazines.

When it's raining, I like watching DVDs.

Grammar

- I like + noun

I like **films**.

- I like + verb + **ing**

I like listen**ing** to music.
I like go**ing** to concerts.
I like swim**ming**.
I like run**ning**.
I like danc**ing**.
I like hav**ing** friends over.

(Note: swim**m**ing, run**n**ing, danc~~e~~ing, hav~~e~~ing)

 Now listen

What will we do tomorrow?

If it's windy, we'll go for a walk.

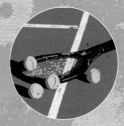

If it's cold on Friday, I won't play tennis.

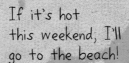

If it's hot this weekend, I'll go to the beach!

If it's warm tomorrow, we'll go swimming.

👋 Try it out!

- Say what you like doing in different weathers.
- What will you do on the weekend? Say what you will do if . . .
  - it's cold
  - it's windy
  - it's warm
  - it's hot

👄 Grammar

You saw in Unit 6 that the present continuous is used to talk about the future (p.40). You can also talk about the future using **will**. This is used when:

- you are talking about something that you think will definitely happen

Don't worry – we **will** be there on time!

- you are talking about something you intend to do in the near future

If I have time this evening, I**'ll surf** the internet.

I **will** go	we **will** go
you **will** go	you **will** go
he/she/it **will** go	they **will** go

I**'ll** go = I **will** go
we**'ll** have = we **will** have

In the negative **will** becomes **won't**: If it rains, I **won't** go out.

Note that the verb in the **If . . .** part of the sentence is in the present tense, even though it refers to the future.

If it**'s** hot this weekend, I'll go to the beach!

👂 **Now listen**

Review 2

1 You're at the train station. Write the questions.

1 train leave – when? _____ When does the next train to Portland leave?_____

2 arrive? _____

3 how long? _____

4 change? _____

5 off-peak ticket – when? _____

6 Denver train? _____

7 platform – leave? _____

8 ticket valid? _____

2 Say what these people are doing next week.

1 Tuesday fly Dallas – Jake _____ Next Tuesday Jake is flying to Dallas._____

2 Friday go gym – Cristina _____

3 Monday study French – Tess _____

4 Sunday nothing – me _____

5 Saturday go out friends – you _____

3 Put the words in the right order.

1 to you drink something like would ? _____ Would you like something to drink?_____

2 yourselves cookies please to help _____

3 sandwich coffee think have a I and I'll _____

4 a cake you of piece like would chocolate ? _____

5 please we'll a house red of the bottle have _____

6 Friday movies the every I to go _____

7 three a week piano I the times play _____

8 weekend friends with my on the out I go _____

9 tonight want you to do watch what ? _____

10 hot we'll if tomorrow, football it's play _____

4 Order in a restaurant.

Answer the waiter using the words given. Prepare your
answers, then listen to the recording and join in. Look
back at Unit 7 if you need help.

- Are you ready to order?
- yes / to start, fish soup

- And for the main course?
- in quiche?

- It's a tart made with leek and cheese.
- good / have that

- Would you like vegetables or a salad with that?
- vegetables / carrots

- And to drink?
- glass house white / bottled water

5 Say what you like doing.

Answer Anna using the words given. Prepare
your answers, then listen to the recording and
join in. Look back at Unit 8 if you need help.

- What do you like doing on the weekend?

- Friday nights / movies / friends   On Friday nights I like going to the movies
with friends.

- Saturday / play tennis

- Sunday / read paper / drink coffee

- What are you doing this weekend?
- go Vancouver

I don't feel well

- Learning body vocabulary
- Saying I feel ill
- Saying what's wrong with me

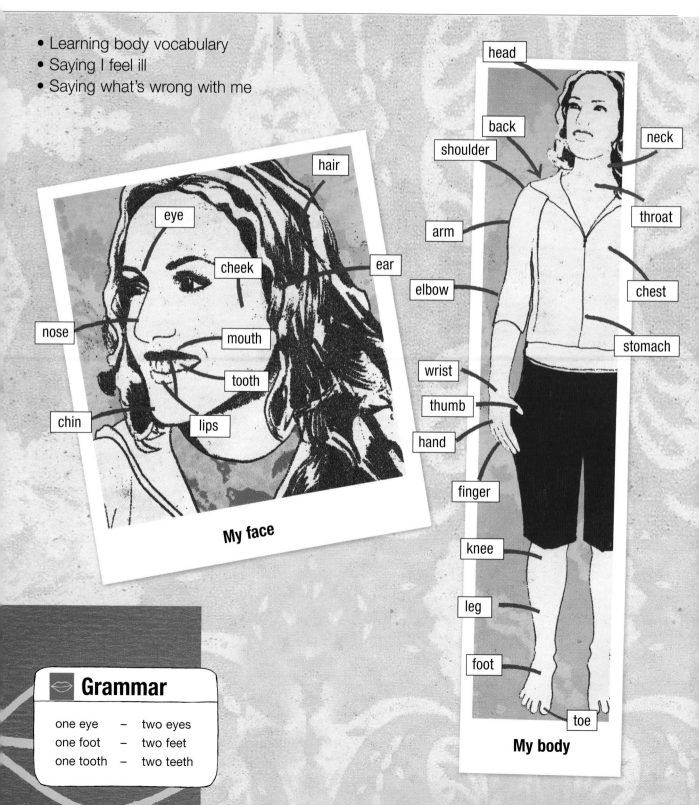

My face

My body

⬭ Grammar

one eye	–	two eyes
one foot	–	two feet
one tooth	–	two teeth

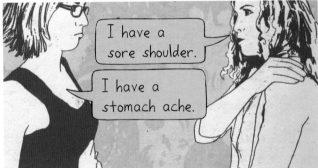

Try it out!

- With your book closed, try to remember the words for all the parts of the body shown on p.58.

- Imagine you're ill. What is wrong with you? How do you feel?

  My head hurts and I feel dizzy.

- Then think about how to talk about other people.

  He feels dizzy.

Tip

If you're feeling ill, you can get help:

- At the pharmacy: you can get advice and a wide range of medicine.

- At the doctor: some medicine needs to be prescribed by a doctor (e.g. antibiotics) – you need to make an appointment.

- At the hospital: if it's an emergency, go straight to a hospital (ER = Emergency Room) or call 911 for an ambulance.

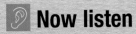 **Now listen**

At the pharmacy

- Describing symptoms
- Asking for and understanding advice
- Buying medicines

👁 Tip

At the pharmacy, the **pharmacist** can advise you on what is wrong with you and what medicine to take. However, he/she can recommend 'over the counter' medicine only (medicine that he/she is authorized to sell).

For stronger medicines, you need to see a doctor first and get a prescription. A pharmacist can then supply the medicine, which you need to pay for.

There are 24-hour pharmacies in many cities. You may want to locate the one in your area.

Could you recommend something for a cold, please?

Of course. What are your symptoms?

My head hurts and I feel very tired. My throat is sore too.

Do you have a fever?

Yes, I think so.

How long have you been ill?

For four days.

It sounds like the flu. I suggest you go home and go to bed. Take these pills three times a day. And don't forget to drink lots of water.

Do I need to see a doctor?

If you don't feel better in a couple of days, make an appointment.

👄 Grammar

Note that the pharmacist uses the imperative, because these are formal instructions: **go**, **take**, **make**. The negative is formed just by putting **don't** in front of the verb: **Don't forget. Don't go to work.**

She also uses some less direct expressions to give advice: **I suggest . . .**, **Make sure you . . .**

Do you have something for a cold/flu/ a headache/hayfever?

a bandage

a tube of cream

Band-Aids

aspirin/ ibuprofen/ Tylenol

cough syrup

throat lozenges   antibiotics

Try it out!

- What would you ask the pharmacist for?
  – You have a headache.

Could I have some aspirin, please?

  – You have a sore throat.
  – You have a cough.
  – You have a small cut on your finger.

Listening task

- What are the customer's symptoms?
- What medicine does the pharmacist suggest?
- What else does he advise?

Grammar

He must not drink with this medicine. = He must not drink alcohol.

Now listen

At the doctor

- Making an appointment
- Explaining symptoms in more detail
- Understanding instructions

Hello. I'd like to make an appointment, please.

Yes — for when?

For today, if possible.

Let's see . . . can you make 4:45 (four forty-five)?

Yes, that would be fine.

And your name is . . . ?

Anna Millar.

Anna Millar. Thank you. That's 4:45 with Dr. Harvey. Wait in the upstairs waiting room and he will call your name.

Grammar

Useful phrases:
Can I make an appointment for . . . ?
my son / daughter / husband / wife
His / Her name is . . .
Do you have an appointment today?
Do you have anything on Friday?

In this context, it's useful to review numbers for times.

Tip

In the U.S., you can also get health advice from a telephone nurse who will advise you on what to do and whether you need to see a doctor. This service is available 24 hours a day. The doctor or hospital will give you details.

 **Now listen**

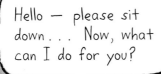

Hello — please sit down . . . Now, what can I do for you?

How long have you had it?

Let's just take a look . . . Ah, yes . . . you have an infection.

I'll give you a prescription for some antibiotics.

Take two pills three times a day, after meals. You need to take them for a week. You should try to rest as much as you can. And don't forget to drink plenty of water. If you don't feel better by the end of the week, come back and see me again.

I have a very sore throat.

Since Monday. My throat is so sore I can't eat. My neck is also very stiff and I feel tired all the time.

How often do I need to take the pills?

👄 Grammar

You can use **you should** or **you need to** to give advice or an instruction:

You should try to rest.

You need to take the pills for a week.

You can also use **please** with the imperative to make an instruction less abrupt:

Please sit down.

Time phrases:

since Monday

three times a day

after meals

for a week

by the end of the week

 Try it out!

- Make an appointment at the doctor's for your daughter – you want one as soon as possible.

- You have the following symptoms. What will you tell the doctor?

started Monday /
headache / nose / dizzy

started weekend / ears
hurt / temperature / been sick

 Listening task

You'll hear a doctor giving three different people some instructions. Listen and note the advice given.

 **Now listen**

Finding out about a job

- Understanding a job advertisement
- Calling to find out more
- Outlining my experience

Tip

In the U.S., websites are a good source for job listings. Many companies post jobs on their websites, and there are job-finding websites that list job opportunities in various subjects. You can also find jobs listed in news-papers and on their websites. If you don't have a computer, you can access the internet in internet cafés or in public libraries.

HELP WANTED

PART-TIME
RECEPTIONIST REQUIRED

Must be experienced in
Word and Excel.

SUMMER SEASON WORKERS

Community center requires summer season workers in the following areas:

- swimming pool
- children's vacation clubs
- gym (adults)

You need to be:

friendly, efficient and willing to work as part of a team.

Good rates of pay.

Working hours negotiable.

RESTAURANT NEEDS

WAITERS/ WAITRESSES

for weekend work

Experience essential

Can you speak
Spanish, French, Italian or German?

Do you enjoy
working with children?

The International School is looking for part-time language instructors for its International Summer Camp to teach campers basic language and culture in fun ways.

Grammar

To talk about something that you did for a time in the past, use **used to**: the form doesn't change, whatever the subject.

You **used to** teach.
He **used to** work as a doctor.
They **used to** live in New York.

I'm looking for a job for the summer. What do you think of this one?

It sounds great. You would get to work with children and to use your languages.

Hello, my name's Jake Ravens. I'm calling about your ad for language instructors in Monday's newspaper. Can you tell me more about the job?

Yes, certainly. We're looking for enthusiastic people who love working with children and teenagers. You must be fluent in English and a second language. Our summer camp activities include games, arts and crafts, and music.

That sounds very interesting.

Do you have experience in this area?

Well, not as a language instructor, but I grew up in Germany and I speak German fluently and some French. I teach Third Grade, so I have experience with children. And I studied piano so I use music in my classroom.

That sounds very useful. If you're interested in applying, I can give you my e-mail address and you could send us your résumé.

Yes, please.

It's p.thomas @. . .

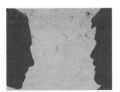 **Tip**

When applying for a job, it's important to present yourself very positively. However, you should also be aware that in general conversation people tend to use expressions which play down their abilities and skills.

I'm **pretty good** at golf.
I'm **not too bad** at French.
I can sing, but **not very well**.

Try it out!

• Pick one of the jobs advertised on p.64. Imagine you call and ask for more details. What questions will you ask?

• Write down 10 sentences about you and your family using **used to**.

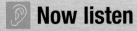 **Now listen**

Applying for a job

- Writing a job application letter
- Asking and answering questions about the past
- Reporting what I did/thought

 **Grammar**

Past simple

You use the past simple to talk about completed actions in the past:

I **went** to France. I **worked** in Germany.

To form the past simple of regular verbs, you add –**ed** to the verb (or –**d** if the verb already ends in –**e**): **worked**, **changed**.

The same form is used for all subjects:

I **worked**, he **worked**, we **worked**, etc.

However, many verbs have irregular past simple forms: you need to learn these by heart. Some of the most important ones are listed here.

buy	**bought**
do	**did**
give	**gave**
go	**went**
have	**had**
say	**said**
see	**saw**
take	**took**
be	**was/were***

*Note the past simple of **to be**: it is the only one with two forms – I **was**, you **were**, he/she/it **was**; we **were**, you **were**, they **were**.

Dear Polly Thomas,

I would like to apply for the position of language instructor, as advertised in the *Morning Herald* on June 8. Please find attached a copy of my résumé.

I grew up in Germany, and four years ago I moved back home to the U.S. I received my teaching degree from Ohio State University. I studied education and music, and I took French classes as well. English is my first language, and I am also fluent in German.

I currently work as a Third Grade teacher, which means I spend a great deal of time with children. I have experience in planning lessons and creative activities that are age-appropriate, and I enjoy helping my students learn and explore. Last year I was in charge of a summer school for high school students and had five teachers working for me.

I am free from the beginning of June. I am looking for a part-time summer job that will allow me to use my teaching degree and to use my language skills. I hope that my résumé is of interest to you and look forward to hearing from you.

Sincerely,

Jake Ravens

Jake Ravens

 **Tip**

In a more formal context (like Jake's job application letter), it's better to use the full forms of verbs: so, **I would like** rather than **I'd like**; **I am free** rather than **I'm free**.

Now listen

Did you send off your application last week?

Yes, I did. The deadline was Friday so I finished it on Thursday night and e-mailed it right away.

What did you say in your letter?

I said that I'm interested in using my teaching degree and that I have experience working with children. I included details of the languages I speak and said I used to study music.

Did you mention that you wanted to work with teenagers in particular?

No, I didn't.

When will you hear if you have an interview?

By next Tuesday, I think.

Grammar

Past simple – question forms

Did you send . . . ?
Yes, I **did**.
No, I **didn't**.

What **did** you say?
I **said** . . .

to be is different:
Were you there?
Was she at the party?

The past tense is also used when you are reporting what someone has said/thought.

I **said** that I was interested in using my degree.

He **thought** that I needed to improve my Spanish.

that is sometimes left out:
I **said** I was interested in using my degree.

 Try it out!

• Give the past tense of these verbs, using what you have learned on these pages:
work, be, go, teach, see, want, tell, have, say.

• Choose one of the ads on p.64 and write a job application letter like Jake's.

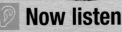 **Now listen**

At an interview

- Preparing for an interview
- Taking part in an interview

 **Tip**

When you're preparing for an interview in English, make some notes using the headings here. The expressions listed will get you started – look up any other vocabulary you need.

You might also want to think about your hobbies and interests (see Unit 8) and your plans for the future (see Unit 12), in case you're asked about those. It's also a good idea to prepare a few questions about the job and/or the company, to show that you're really interested.

Qualifications

I have a degree in . . .
English
French
marketing
engineering
math
law
history
psychology
sociology

Reasons for wanting the job

I enjoy working with . . .
the public
children
animals

I would like the opportunity to . . .
work abroad/travel
develop my management skills

Work experience

I worked in a call center for two years.
I taught English in Bulgaria for six months.
I managed the store when my boss was away.

Skills

I am fluent in French.
My Spanish is good — I can cope in everyday situations.

I work well . . .
with young people
as part of a team

I'm good . . .
at meeting deadlines
at managing budgets
with customers

I have a clean driving record.

Now listen

I'm good at teaching, and I've learned a lot about German language and culture, which I enjoy sharing with others.

Why do you want to work as a language instructor?

How good are your languages?

I'm fluent in German. I'm not quite as strong in French, but I studied it in college. When I went to France on vacation, I didn't have any problems getting by and communicating.

You used to study music too, didn't you?

Yes, I studied piano for two years. After that I decided to concentrate on elementary education. I was able to teach children many subjects, including music.

You certainly have the kind of experience we're looking for. Thank you for coming in. We'll be in touch.

Grammar

Past simple – negative

I **didn't have** any problems.
He **doesn't** want to go yet.

to be is different:
I **wasn't** there last night.
They **weren't** at home.

Note the tag question **didn't you?**, etc.: this comes up a lot when you use the past simple.

You **called** him this morning, **didn't you?**

He went to America, **didn't he?**

It is also used with used to:
You used to teach, **didn't you?**
They said they wanted to come, **didn't they?**

Try it out!

- Prepare some notes for an interview in English, using a dictionary for any words which aren't covered here.

Listening task

- What job is Neela applying for?
- Why does she want it?
- What experience does she have?
- What three skills does she mention?

 Now listen

Returning something

- Explaining a problem
- Asking for a refund / an exchange

There's a problem with this / these.

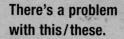

There's a mark / hole.
A button / piece is missing.

I'd like to return this / these.
Here's the receipt.

It's faulty. / It isn't working. / It's broken.

I bought it here / in your Eastside store . . .
last week / last month / a few weeks ago.

It's too small / big.

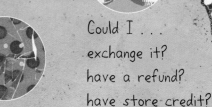

Could I . . .
exchange it?
have a refund?
have store credit?

I got it as a present.
I don't have the receipt.

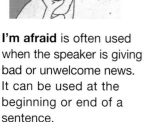

👁 Tip

I'm afraid is often used when the speaker is giving bad or unwelcome news. It can be used at the beginning or end of a sentence.

I'm afraid I can't come to your party.

You would have to pay, **I'm afraid**.

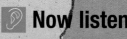 **Now listen**

Excuse me. There's a problem with this necklace. I bought it here in January and the catch is broken. Could I exchange it?

How long would that take?

Let's see . . . ah, yes. We can't exchange it, I'm afraid — you bought it too long ago. But we could mend it for you.

Three to four weeks.

I'd really like it back sooner than that.

There's a jeweller around the corner that does repairs. You could take it there. They might be able to do it more quickly.

And you'll pay for that?

We would do the repair free of charge, but if you got it mended somewhere else, I'm afraid you would have to pay.

Grammar

would (or its short form **'d**)

Offers
Would you like a replacement?
How much **would** you like?

Polite requests
I'd really like it back sooner than that.
I **would** like some coffee.

would is also used for *hypothetical situations* – often with **if**, though this is sometimes just understood.

We **would** do the repair free of charge (if you wanted us to).
(If you got it mended somewhere else) you **would** have to pay.

could

Polite requests
Could you help me?
Could I exchange it?

Options
We **could** repair it for you or you **could** take it to the jeweller.

Try it out!

• You need to return three things that you're not happy with. Use the notes to make up three conversations.

watch/bought last week; strap broken/refund?

shirt/bought yesterday; button missing/exchange?

T-shirt/present; no receipt; store credit?

Listening task

• What is the man returning?
• What's the problem with it?
• What does he want?

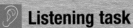

Reporting a loss

- Explaining that something is missing
- Giving information

handbag

backpack

wallet

purse

suitcase

I've lost my . . .

Tip

If you lose something in a station or airport, or on public transportation, try asking for it at the **Lost and Found** on site.

If you lose something in the street, or don't know where you lost it, you can report this to a police station.

You'll need to be prepared to describe what you have lost, when you last had it and where you think you lost it.

My . . . has been stolen is another useful expression in this context.

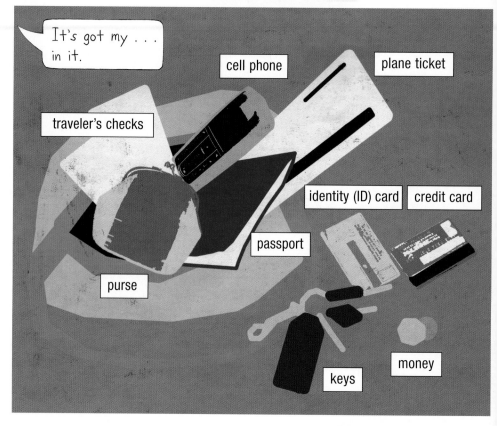

It's got my . . . in it.

cell phone

plane ticket

traveler's checks

identity (ID) card

credit card

passport

purse

keys

money

 **Now listen**

Can you describe the bag?

I'm afraid no one has handed in a bag like that today. If I could take some more details . . . When did you last have it?

And what is in the bag?

If you could give me your name and telephone number, we'll contact you if it turns up.

It's a red leather backpack — a small one.

I had it when I got on the train — I was on the 9:40 from St. Louis. I bought a newspaper . . . I might have left it by the newspaper kiosk. I definitely didn't have it when I went to pay in the café.

It's got my purse and my keys in it. . . . oh, and my cell phone.

Try it out!

- Imagine you have lost your bag and you need to go to the Lost and Found.

  – Describe your bag.

  – Say when you last had it.

  I last had it . . .

  – Say what's in it.

  – Give your contact information (name, address, phone number).

 Grammar

This topic involves another verb tense used when talking about the past (the present perfect) – **I've lost my passport.** You've seen some examples of this tense already in some of the English instructions and information. It will not be covered in detail in the course: at this stage, it's best just to learn the key phrases by heart when you come across them.

 **Now listen**

Solving other problems

- Changing travel arrangements
- Finding out what has happened

Now listen

Try it out!

- You slept in and missed your train! Using the following information, arrange to change your ticket:

missed 9:15 — next 11:30

- You're at the airport. One of your suitcases has arrived, but not the other. Find out what has happened, using the following information.

6:10 from Detroit; changed in Houston

blue leather suitcase

you're traveling around, but will be in Santa Fe for 3 days

 **Now listen**

Sharing plans

- Talking about what I usually do
- Talking about future plans
- Asking people about their plans

My favorite season's spring — winter really depresses me!

I like summer most of all: I'm going to have lots of barbecues and invite all my friends over.

I prefer autumn to summer — I don't like it too hot.

Winter's the best season for outdoor activities — skiing, snowboarding . . . And I really love Christmas!

👄 Grammar

in (the)
spring / summer / autumn / winter

last spring . . .
this spring . . .
next spring . . .

during the spring . . .

 **Now listen**

Are you going away this summer, Anna?

I'm working in Chicago for two weeks — I'm hoping to go on vacation after that.

Where are you going?

I'm thinking of going to Italy — maybe Sicily. What about you?

I might go to Mexico.

Who with?

Tom. If Paul can get the time off work, he says he might come too.

He works too hard, doesn't he? When would you go?

Probably in September.

And where would you stay?

I might not stay at the same hotel as last time — it was really expensive. Do you know anywhere good?

Yes — I stayed in a hotel in Cancun that was fantastic. I've got the name on my computer . . . Why don't you try it?

Thanks. How much was it? I don't want anything too expensive . . .

👄 Grammar

Phrases to use when you're not completely sure about what you're going to do:

I'm hoping to go . . .
I'm thinking of going . . .
I might go . . .

And in questions:
When **would** you go?
Where **would** you stay?
(Compare: When **are** you **going**? and Where **are** you **staying**? if the plan is more definite.)

✋ Try it out!

- Write a question using each of the following question words:
  what, who, when, where, why, how.

- What are your plans for the summer? Write them out, making clear which are definite (**I'm going to . . . /I will . . .**) and which you're less sure about (**I'm hoping to . . .**).

- Do the same for the rest of your family/your friends.

 Now listen

Future intentions

- Thinking further ahead
- Talking about my plans in more detail

👄 Grammar

You use the present continuous tense (or the future tense) to talk about what is going to happen in the future. However, in the part of the sentence which focuses on time, you use the **present simple**. Look out for the words **when**, **before** or **after** to remind you (compare If . . . in Unit 8, p.55):

When I **leave** school, I'm going to work abroad.

I'll be President before I**'m** forty.

Note the use of the **future tense** to show you think something will definitely happen:

. . . **I'll be** President.

Before I'm forty, . . .

I'd like to go back to college.

I don't know what I want to do.

I'd like to get a new job.

I want to start my own business.

If I have a baby, . . .

I'm going to work abroad.

I'll be very rich.

👄 Tip

Now that you know a lot of English, you can start to think more about how you say things. Using longer sentences can make what you say more interesting – and also help structure your thoughts.

Join simple statements using words like **and**, **but**, **because**, **although**, etc. Think about the order things happen and use words like **when**, **before**, **first**, **then**, **later**, etc.

✋ Try it out!

- Think up five future plans for yourself. Try to start each one differently, using some of the beginnings on pp.78–79 for ideas. Use a dictionary and try to come up with other ideas.

👂 Listening task

Listen to the five people.

- What do they want to do and when?

👂 Now listen

Reading for detail

- Understanding a more difficult text
- Using what I know

Win a vacation to California!

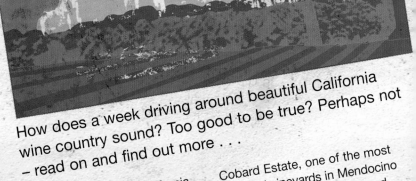

How does a week driving around beautiful California wine country sound? Too good to be true? Perhaps not – read on and find out more . . .

Mendocino County, California, famous for producing the finest organic wines, is the perfect place to have a vacation – and we're going to give you the chance to experience it. Why not take part in our competition to win a week's vacation for two there? The lucky couple will fly to San Francisco, where they will spend the night in a luxury hotel. Next day they will pick up a rental car and drive to the

Cobard Estate, one of the most beautiful vineyards in Mendocino County, where they will spend four days in one of the lovely 19th-century guest houses on site. They will be given a guided tour of the vineyard, famous for its organic red, white and rosé wines, and be shown in detail how its prize-winning white wine Cobard Viognier is made.

 Grammar

As you saw in Unit 4 (p.28), the **comparative** is used to compare two things. When you want to compare more than two things, you use the superlative:

pretty   prettier
the prettiest

beautiful   more beautiful
the most beautiful

the prettiest town **in** the state

The **superlative** is formed in a similar way to the comparative: for shorter adjectives, the ending **–est** is added; for longer ones, use **the most** + the adjective. Remember that adjectives ending in **y** change this to **i** before the **–est** ending is added.

There are a few irregular adjectives:

good   better   **the best**
bad   worse   **the worst**

The estate also includes a ten-acre garden. The fruit, vegetables and herbs grown here – all organic – supply the vineyard restaurant, rated one of the best restaurants in the country. Our winners will get the chance to enjoy the restaurant's famous food and ambience during their stay.

After four days at the vineyard, our winners will round off their trip with a couple of days sightseeing in the area. Not only is Mendocino one of the prettiest seaside towns in the state, it is also situated within an easy drive of five state parks, with their beautiful plants and wildlife.

Our winners will spend two nights in Norton House, a tranquil hotel on the edge of one of the parks, before a final night in San Francisco. What could be better?

It couldn't be easier to take part. To win, all you need to do is answer this question:

Which color is Cobard Estate's most famous wine?

> Let's go for it. You never know — we might win . . .

Tip

The article contains some vocabulary and structures you aren't familiar with. Don't look up every new word: use what you do know to work out enough to understand the general idea of the text. Think about:

Words that look like words you already know in English or your own language.

Words you can guess from the context (e.g. ten-**acre** garden; red, white and **rosé** wine).

Use the questions in the **Try it out!** section too: they'll help you focus on the key points and in this way may make some details clearer.

Try it out!

• Read the text again and answer the questions.

1 What is the prize?

2 How many people is the prize for?

3 Where do the winners fly to?

4 How do they get to Mendocino County?

5 What kind of wine does the estate produce?

6 Why is the estate restaurant famous?

7 What will the winners do in the last few days?

8 What is the answer to the competition question?

Review 3

1 Complete the questions

with *why, when, where, who, how* or *what*.

1 _____ would you like to do when you finish your degree?

2 _____ are you going on vacation with?

3 _____ did you decide to get a new job?

4 _____ will you stay?

5 _____ much does it cost?

6 _____ do you want to take a year off?

2 Put the words in the right order

1 very throat tired hurts and I my feel

2 said in interested I that I using was degree my

3 I'd make my appointment please to like for an wife

4 you to home go go and suggest I bed

5 became for piano I before teacher I a studied

6 insect have for you something do bites

7 music study to piano classroom use
   used in I my so I

3 Complete the sentences

with the correct form of the verb in the past simple tense.

1 I [not/buy] any shoes.

   I didn't buy any shoes.

2 I (work) for two years in London.

3 He (go) out with friends on Friday night.

4 Last year she [has] ten people working for her.

5 We [say] that we didn't know where the bar was.

6 They [decide] to go to the movies.

7 You [not/give] it to me.

8 I [see] Bill yesterday.

9 I [not/be] very happy to see him.

10 [be] he on vacation last week?

4 Take part in an interview

Answer the interviewer using the words given. Prepare your answers,
then listen to the recording and join in. Look back at Unit 10 if you need help.

• Why do you want to work with us here at the recreation center?

— love sports — good with the public/children — opportunity
to learn other sports

• Do you have any experience?

— work — year — recreation center Spain;
taught swimming — two years

5 Report a loss

Reply using the words given. Prepare your answers, then listen to
the recording and join in. Look back at Unit 11 if you need help.

• How can I help you?

— lost bag — green, small

• When did you last have it?

— this morning — left in the restroom?

• What is in the bag?

— cell phone, credit card, keys

6 Ask Anna about her plans

Ask Anna what she's going to do this summer, using the words given. Prepare your
answers, then listen to the recording and join in. Look back at Unit 12 if you need help.

— go away — autumn?
• I'm going to New York.

— who with?
• With Jake.

— when?
• We're going at the end of October.

— where — stay?
• We're staying at a nice hotel right in Manhattan.

Grammar

Nouns

In English, nouns have no gender: this means that the words that go with nouns, such as articles (**the** or **a**) and adjectives, do not change form depending on the noun.

a becomes **an** before a vowel sound: **an apple**.

Plurals

To make most nouns plural, add **–s** (apple, apple**s**). Some are irregular:

man	men
woman	women
child	children
foot	feet
tooth	teeth

Possession

Anna**'s** holiday; the girl**s'** friends

Countable/Uncountable nouns

Nouns are either countable (apple, boy, etc.) or uncountable (water, rice, etc.). Uncountable nouns are never used with numbers, with **a/an** or as plurals. (Compare **apple**: two apple**s**, an apple.)

How **much** cheese would you like?
How **many** apples would you like?

some, **any** and **a lot of** can be used for countable and uncountable nouns:

I'd like **some** cheese/apples.
Do you have **any** cheese/apples?
She buys **a lot of** cheese/apples.

Pronouns

You use a pronoun instead of a noun when it is clear what you mean.

Subject pronouns

I, you (singular), he, she, it; we, you (plural), they
We saw Tom on Tuesday.

Object pronouns

me, you (singular), him, her, it; us, you (plural), them
Kate saw **them** last week.

Possessive pronouns

mine, yours (singular), his, hers, its; ours, yours (plural), theirs

Here's my phone number. Can I have **yours?** (= your phone number)

Demonstrative pronouns

this (one), that (one); these (ones), those (ones)
I like **this**, but I prefer **that one** over there.

Adjectives

Adjectives tell you more about a noun. They are the same for singular items and plural items. They come before the noun or after the verb **to be**.

a **red** coat – it's **red**
blue jeans – they're **blue**

When you are comparing two things, you use the *comparative* form of the adjective + **than**.

A toy is **cuter than** a bag.
A watch is **more useful than** a necklace.

To form the comparative:
Short adjectives add **–er–** (adjectives ending in **–y** change this to **–i –**):

cheap – cheap**er**; pretty – prett**ier**

Long adjectives use **more**:
expensive – **more** expensive

good and **bad** have irregular comparatives:
better, **worse**

When you are comparing more than two things, you use the superlative:

the **prettiest** town in the state

To form the superlative:

cheap – cheap**er** – cheap**est**
pretty – pretti**er** – the pretti**est**
expensive – **more** expensive – **the most** expensive

good and **bad** have irregular superlatives:
the best, the worst

Possessive adjectives

my, your (singular), his/her/its; our, your (plural), their

I phoned **my** brother.

Demonstrative adjectives

this, that; these, those

These necklaces are pretty, but **those**
necklaces are prettier.

Verbs

*Note: Only the **I** form is given here for reference.*

Present

In English, there are two forms of the present tense:
the *present simple* and the *present continuous*.

Present simple

The **present simple** is used for things that happen
regularly or for *facts*.

On Mondays I **go** to the gym.
I **like** swimming.

The present simple verb form for I/you/we/they is the
same as the infinitive (i.e. the verb form you find listed
in the dictionary): **work** – I **work**, they **work**

For the **he/she/it** form of most verbs, add **–s**:
he/she/it **works**

Note the following irregular verbs:
have (he/she/it **has**)
be (I **am**, you **are**, he/she/it **is**; we **are**,
you **are**, they **are**)
(The short forms of the verb **be** are common in spoken
English: I**'m**, you**'re**, he**'s**, she**'s**, it**'s**, we**'re**, they**'re**)

Present simple negative: I don't like;
he/she it **doesn't** like
Present simple questions: **do** I like?;
does he/she/it like?
+ *short answer:* yes, I **do**; no, I **don't**;
yes, he/she/it **does**; no, he/she/it **doesn't**

Present continuous

The **present continuous** is used for things that are
happening *right now*.

I**'m calling** about the language classes.
Are you **looking** for a French course?

It is also used to talk about the *future*.

I**'m meeting** him there.
On Monday, she**'s going** to the gym.

The present continuous is formed with the present
simple of **to be** + **–ing** form of the verb.

I**'m flying** direct to Rome.
We**'re seeing** him on Sunday.

Present continuous negative: I'm **not** coming;
he/she/it **isn't** coming

Present continuous questions: **am** I coming?;
is he/she/it coming?
+ *short answer:* yes, I **am**; no, I**'m not**;
yes, he/she/it **is**; no, he/she/it **isn't**

Past

English uses a number of tenses to talk about the past.
This course focuses on the **past simple**.

Past simple

You use the past simple to talk about completed actions
in the past.

I **went** to Mexico. I **worked** in Spain.

To form the past simple of regular verbs, you add **–ed**
to the verb (or **–d** if the verb already ends in **–e**):
worked, **changed**.

The same form is used for all subjects: **I worked**,
he worked, **we worked**, etc.

However, many verbs have irregular past simple forms: you need to learn these by heart. Here are a few of the most useful ones.

buy – **bought**
do – **did**
give – **gave**
go – **went**
have – **had**
say – **said**
see – **saw**
take – **took**
be – **was/were***

*Note the past simple of **to be**: it is the only one with two forms – I was, you were, he/she/it was; we were, you were, they were.

Past simple negative: I **didn't** work

Past simple questions: **did** I work?
+ *short answer*: yes, I **did**; no, I **didn't**

Future

The present continuous is used to talk about the future (p.78). You can also talk about the future using *will*. This is used when:

• you are talking about something that you think will definitely happen.

  Don't worry – **we will** be there on time!

• you are talking about something you intend to do in the near future.

  If I have time this evening, I**'ll surf** the internet.

To form the future, you use **will** + verb. The same form is used for all subjects: **I will work**, **we will work**. Note that **will** is often shortened to **'ll**, especially in spoken English.

I **will go**   we **will go**
you **will go**   you **will go**
he/she/it **will go**   they **will go**

Future negative: I **won't** work
Future simple questions: **will** I work?
+ *short answer*: yes, I **will**; no, I **won't**

Usage

You use the present continuous tense or the future tense to talk about what is going to happen in the future. However, in the part of the sentence which focuses on time, you use the **present simple**. Look out for words like **when**, **before** or **after** to remind you.

When I **leave** school, I'm going to work abroad.

I'll be President before I**'m** forty.

Questions

For information on how to form questions, see under the different verb tenses, pp.85–86.

Note also the forms for tag questions:
is ⟶ **isn't he/she/it?**
are ⟶ **aren't you?**, etc.

Present simple
He plays tennis, **doesn't he?**
They go to the movies every week, **don't they?**

Past simple
You bought that on vacation, **didn't you?**
They spoke English fluently, **didn't they?**

Extra

For **the numbers 1–1000+**, see pp.9, 11 and 22.
For **the numbers 1st, 2nd, 3rd**, etc., see p.35.

For **the days of the week**, see p.32.
For **the months of the year**, see p.34.
For **dates**, see p.35.
For **the seasons of the year**, see p.76.
For **times**, see pp.34 and 37.
For **further time phrases**, see pp.38 and 39.

 # Answers/Transcript

Answers to Review sections

Review 1, pp.30–31 (Track 17)

1
1 I **have** two brothers.
2 My name**'s** Anna.
3 I **like** it very much.
4 We **are** Jake's parents.
5 Where **are** you from?
6 She**'s** English.
7 This **is** my friend Amir.
8 He **works** in a hospital.
9 I**'m** a photographer.
10 **Is there** a grocery store near here?

2
1 chicken
2 cookies
3 tomatoes
4 strawberries
5 orange juice
6 bag of candy
7 box of chocolates
8 bottle of wine
9 pound of grapes
10 carton of milk

3
1 I'm Spanish. I speak Spanish.
2 I'm Chinese. I speak Chinese.
3 I'm Russian. I speak Russian.
4 I'm American. I speak English.
5 I'm Brazilian. I speak Portuguese.

4
1 My name's . . .
2 I'm . . .
3 My phone number is . . .
4 My address is . . .
5 I'm from . . .
6 No, I'm . . .
7 Yes, I'm married. / No, I'm . . .
8 Yes, I do. / No, I live in . . .
9 I'm a . . .
10 Yes, it's . . . / No, it's . . .

5
1 Is there a pharmacy near here?
2 How do you get to the bus station?
3 Go along this road to the stoplight.
4 Then take the second right.
5 Is this the right bus for the Science Museum?
6 I'd like some grapes, please.

7 I like it very much.
8 Do you have them in a size 8?
9 Can I try them in orange, please?
10 This CD is more interesting than that one.

6
• Can I help you?
– **I'm looking for a present for my brother.**
• What does he like?
– **He likes CDs and DVDs.**
• What about this DVD? It's very exciting.
– **No, it's not his thing. What about that one? Is that one good?**
• That one is even better. It's more exciting.
– **How much is it?**
• This one costs $19.99.
– **That's expensive. Do you have anything cheaper?**
• This DVD is cheaper and it's more interesting than the first one.
– **I'll take it. Thank you very much.**

Review 2, pp.56–57 (Track 34)

1
1 When does the next train to . . . leave?
2 When does it arrive?
3 How long does it take?
4 Do I have to change?
5 When can I use an off-peak ticket?
6 Is this the Denver train?
7 Which platform does it leave from?
8 Is this ticket valid on this train?

2
1 Next Tuesday Jake is flying to Dallas.
2 Next Friday Cristina is going to the gym.
3 Next Monday Sara is studying French.
4 Next Sunday I am doing nothing.
5 Next Saturday you are going out with friends.

3
1 Would you like something to drink?
2 Please help yourselves to cookies.
3 I think I'll have a sandwich and coffee.
4 Would you like a piece of chocolate cake?
5 We'll have a bottle of house red, please.

6 I go to the movies every Friday.
7 I play the piano three times a week.
8 I go out with my friends at the weekend.
9 What do you want to watch tonight?
10 If it's hot tomorrow, we'll play football.

4
• Are you ready to order?
– **Yes, I think so. To start, I'll have the fish soup**.
• And for the main course?
– **What's in a quiche?**
• It's a tart made with leek and cheese.
– **That sounds good. I'll have that.**
• Would you like vegetables or a salad with that?
– **Vegetables – the carrots, please.**
• And to drink?
– **I'll have a glass of house white and a glass of bottled water.**

5
• What do you like doing on the weekend?
– **On Friday nights I like going to the movies with friends.**
– **On Saturdays I like playing tennis.**
– **On Sundays I like reading the paper and drinking coffee.**
• What are you doing this weekend?
– **I'm going to Vancouver.**

Review 3, pp.82–83 (Track 51)

1
1 **What** would you like to do when you finish your degree?
2 **Who** are you going on vacation with?
3 **Why/When** did you decide to get a new job?
4 **Where** will you stay?
5 **How** much does it cost?
6 **Why/When** do you want to take a year off?

2
1 I feel very tired and my throat hurts.
2 I said that I was interested in using my degree.
3 I'd like to make an appointment for my wife, please.
4 I suggest you go home and go to bed.
5 I studied piano before I became a teacher.

6 Do you have something for insect bites?
7 I used to study piano so I use music in my classroom.

3

1 I **didn't buy** any shoes.
2 I **worked** for two years in London.
3 He **went** out with friends on Friday night.
4 Last year she **had** ten people working for her.
5 We **said** that we didn't know where the bar was.
6 They **decided** to go to the movies.
7 You **did not give** it to me.
8 I **saw** Bill yesterday.
9 I **was not** very happy to see him.
10 **Was** he on vacation last week?

4

• Why do you want to work with us here at the recreation center?
– **I love sports. I'm good with the public and I enjoy working with children. I would like the opportunity to learn other sports.**
• Do you have any experience?
– **I worked for a year in a recreation center in Spain. I have taught swimming for two years.**

5

• How can I help you?
– **I've lost my bag. It's a green bag – quite small.**
• When did you last have it?
– **I had it this morning. I might have left it in the restroom.**

• What is in the bag?
– **It's got my cell phone, my credit card and my keys in it.**

6

– **Are you going away this autumn?**
• I'm going to New York.
– **Who (are you going) with?**
• With Jake.
– **When are you going?**
• We're going at the end of October.
– **Where are you staying?**
• We're staying at a nice hotel in Manhattan.

Listening tasks

Unit 1 (Track 4)
829-4735
265-1147
383-5699

Unit 2 (Track 8)
Yes, he does.
No, she doesn't.
Yes, she does.
Yes, he does.
No, she doesn't.

Unit 3 (Track 11)
Take the first left, then go straight to the grocery store. Turn right and then take the third road after the stoplight. There's a pharmacy on the left.

Unit 4 (Track 14)
4 ounces of grapes,
6 oranges, a pound of carrots,
a carton of apple juice,
2 bags of rice
$11.75

Unit 5 (Track 21)
Japanese class (beginner)
Monday 6:30pm–8:15pm
September 5
$45 a term

Unit 6 (Track 25)
a single room
(Thursday) June 4 to (Tuesday) June 9
$105 a night

Unit 7 (Track 27)
Man: a glass of white wine; nothing
Woman: a glass of red wine; pizza

Unit 8 (Track 32)
a program about Mozart at 8:00pm
a game show at 6:30pm
The Motorcycle Diaries/a movie about Latin America at 9:15pm
Woman likes game shows and movies
Man likes movies

Unit 9 (Track 37)
headache, her throat hurts, she feels achy
aspirin or ibuprofen
stay in bed and drink lots of water

(Track 39)
Take the pills twice a day, morning and evening. Use the cream four times a day.
Give your son the cough syrup three times a day, before meals.
Don't go to work – stay in bed.
Stay warm and drink lots of water. Ibuprofen will make you feel less achy.

Unit 10 (Track 43)
waitress
She wants to stay in New York and to improve her English.
She used to work in a bar when she was in college.
She's friendly, good with people and can remember the orders easily.

Unit 11 (Track 45)
a clock
the alarm is faulty
a refund

Unit 12 (Track 50)
go to college; when she finishes high school
be head of marketing; in 2 years
do volunteer work abroad; when he's 30
start his own business; when he finishes his degree
open a second store; before she has children

Transcript

Unit 1

(Track 1)
Meeting people, pp.6–7
I'm Anna.
What's your name?
My name's Jake.
She's Anna.
He's Jake.

How are you?
I'm fine, thanks.
And you?

Hello!
Hi!
Good morning.
Good afternoon.
Good evening.
Goodnight.
Goodbye!
Bye!
See you soon!

(Track 2)
My family, pp.8–9
I have two sisters.
He has one brother and
two sisters.
She has one son and two
daughters.
my mother and my father
his sister and his brother
her son and her daughter
1, 2, 3, 4, 5, 6, 7, 8, 9, 10

(Track 3)
**More about my family,
pp.10–11**
We're Jake's grandparents.
We're retired.
I'm Jake's cousin Ben.
I live on my own.
I'm Jake's cousin Tina.
I'm in school.
My aunt works in a hospital.
She's a doctor.
My uncle works in a store.
He sells computers.

What's your phone number?
It's 372-9481.
Yes, that's right.
11, 12, 13, 14, 15, 16, 17, 18,
19, 20

What's your address?
It's 523 Oak Street.

Unit 2

(Track 5)
Where I'm from, pp.12–13
I'm from the United States.
Where are you from?
I'm from England.
I'm from Spain.
I'm from Egypt.
I'm from China.

I'm American.
I'm English.
I'm Spanish.
I'm Egyptian.
I'm Chinese.

I speak Spanish.
I speak French and Japanese.
I speak English and Arabic.

This is my friend Cristina.
Hi, Cristina. Pleased to meet
you.
Pleased to meet you too.

You're American, is that right?
Yes.
You're Spanish, aren't you?
That's right.
It's a great party, isn't it?
Yes, it is.

(Track 6)
More about me, pp.14–15
Do you live in New York?
Yes, I do.
No, I don't.
I live in the country.
I live in the city.

Are you married?
Yes, I am.
No, I'm not.

My husband's name is Marco.
He works at the university.
We live near Chicago.
We have two children.
They're in school.
Katie's in grade school. She's
in Fourth Grade.
Paolo's in high school. He's in
Ninth Grade.
Katie likes school, but Paolo
doesn't like it.
I work too. I teach French.
School starts at nine and
finishes at three.

(Track 7)
What I do, pp.16–17
What do you do?
I'm a journalist.
I'm a photographer.
I'm a doctor.
I'm a musician.
I'm an accountant.
I work in a store.
I work in an office.
He's in marketing.
She's in politics.

Do you work?
I'm unemployed.
I look after my children.
I'm a student.
I'm retired.
I'm still in school.

Do you like your job?
I like it very much. It's really
interesting!
Yes, I do.
It's OK.
It's not very interesting.
No, I don't. I don't like it at all!

Unit 3

(Track 9)
**Asking about places,
pp.18–19**
Where I live, there's a movie
theater, a swimming pool, a
school and a bus station. There
isn't a library or a subway
station. And there aren't any
stores.

The museum's very near.
The grocery store's quite far.
The hotel is opposite the city
hall.
The library is next to the
shopping mall.
The post office is between the
parking lot and the movie theater.

Is there a café near here?
Yes, there is.
No, there isn't.

Are there restrooms
near here?
Yes, there are.
No, there aren't.

Is it far?
No, it's near.

About two minutes' walk.
Thanks for your help!
You're welcome.

(Track 10)
**Asking for directions,
pp.20–21**
Excuse me.
How do you get to the train
station?
Turn right.
Go straight.
Take the first right.
Take the second left.
Go straight.
Turn left.

Cross the intersection.
Go over the bridge.
It's on the right.
It's on the left.
on the corner
at the end of the road

I'm sorry, I didn't catch that.
Could you say it again, please?
Could you speak more slowly,
please?

thank you
thank you very much
thanks
many thanks

Don't mention it.
You're welcome.
No problem!

(Track 12)
How I travel, pp.22–23
I go by bike.
I go by bus.
I go by train.
I go by car.
I go on foot.

20, 30, 40, 50, 60, 70, 80, 90,
100
21, 32, 43, 54, 65, 76, 87, 98,
109

Excuse me.
Is this the right bus for the
Science Museum?
Which bus goes downtown?
You can take the number 43.

Is this the right line for the
Science Museum?
You need to catch the blue
line.

Unit 4

(Track 13)
Buying food, pp.24–25
I'd like some apples, please.
I'd like a box of chocolates, please.
I'd like a bottle of red wine and a bag of chips, please.

a pound of apples
half a pound of grapes
4 ounces of cheese

a bag of cookies
a bar of chocolate
a pint of strawberries

a carton of milk
a bottle of water

149, 200, 350, 490, 1000, 1425

Do you have any oranges?
Do you have any bottled water?

What would you like?
I'll have half a pound of grapes.
And some apples, please.
How many would you like?
I'll have four of those.
Anything else?
That's everything, thanks.
That's eleven dollars and seventy-five cents.
That's 8.25 change.

(Track 15)
Buying clothes, pp.26–27
some blue jeans
a pink skirt
a black jacket
green pants

It's orange
It's white
They're yellow
They're brown

small, too small, very small, big, too big, very big.

I'm a size 8.
Do you have them in a size 8?
small
medium
large
extra large
It's a good fit.

I'm looking for some shoes.

Can you help me, please?
Can I see the blue, please?
Can I try them on?
I'll take them, thanks.

(Track 16)
Buying presents, pp.28–29
It's a present.
a pretty necklace
an interesting book
a cute toy
some delicious candy
an expensive bottle of wine
a good CD

A toy is cuter than a bag.
A watch is more useful than a necklace.

Look at this one.
That one's boring.
I prefer these ones.
Those ones are more interesting.
Is this good?
What about that?
Do you like these?
Those are pretty.

Unit 5

(Track 18)
Getting information, pp.32–33
Monday, Tuesday, Wednesday, Thursday, Friday, Saturday, Sunday
on Mondays, on Saturdays

I'm calling about the language classes.
I'm interested in Spanish.
When does it start?
How much does it cost?
That sounds great. Thank you.

It's two o'clock.
It's four o'clock.
It starts at seven o'clock and finishes at nine o'clock.

Hello, is that . . . ?
I'm sorry, I've got the wrong number.
I think you must have the wrong number.

(Track 19)
Signing up, pp.34–35
January, February, March, April, May, June, July, August,

September, October, November, December
My birthday is in March.
I'm starting a class in January.

It's quarter to four.
It's nine-thirty.
It's twenty-five past six.
It's five to twelve.

I'm calling about your salsa dance class.
When is it?
At what time?
Are there spaces still available?
I'm a complete beginner – does that matter?
Can I sign up, please?

on January 1st, on March 3rd, on August 12th

(Track 20)
Giving information, pp.36–37
A B C D E F G H I J K L M N O
P Q R S T U V W X Y Z

I'd like to sign my son up for some lessons.
in the advanced class
Paolo – that's P – A – O – L – O . . .
He's thirteen.
So, the course starts on Friday the 22nd at 4:30?
And it runs for 8 weeks?

Unit 6

(Track 22)
Traveling by train, pp.38–39
I need to get to the city by 9:30.
Do you have a schedule?
Is there a train that leaves about 8?
When is the next train?
How long does it take?
When does it arrive?
Do I have to change?

A day return to Denver, please.
When can I use an off-peak ticket?
On the 3:40.
Which platform does it leave from?
Is this the Denver train?
Is this ticket valid on this train?

(Track 23)
At the airport, pp.40–41
I'm going to Boston for the weekend.
He's flying direct to New York.
I'm meeting him there.
What are you doing this weekend?
I'm seeing some friends for a drink tonight.
Tomorrow I'm playing football.
I'm going to a movie tonight.

Here you are.
I'm checking just one bag.
I'm taking this one on as a carry-on.
Yes, I did.
I packed my bag myself.
A window seat, please.

(Track 24)
Making a reservation, pp.42–43
I'd like to book a room, please.
From November 9th to the 12th.
A double room, please.
A single room.
A room for four people.
How much is it?
Is breakfast included?
I'll take it.

I'd like to book a table for tonight.
for Saturday
for six people
Around 7:30?
8:30's fine.
My name's Millar.

Unit 7

(Track 26)
Visiting a friend, pp.44–45
Would you like to come over for coffee?
Thanks – I'd love to!
I'm sorry, I can't.

Would you like tea or coffee?
Would you like some more cake?
Some more tea?
I'll have coffee, please.
Could I have tea, please?
Yes, please . . . It's delicious!
Thank you.
No, thanks. I'm fine.

Can I get you a drink?
What would you like?
What about you?
Would you like something to drink?
I'll have a glass of red wine.
Just a glass of sparkling water, please.

(Track 28)
Ordering in a café, pp.46–47
She's hungry.
He's thirsty.
I'm really cold!
I'm very hot!

Could we see a menu, please?
What are you having?
I think I'll have coffee and a sandwich.
What about you?
I can't decide.
I don't think I feel like a snack.
What about some cake?
That sounds good.
A cappuccino and a salmon bagel, please.
I'll have an espresso and a piece of chocolate cake.

(Track 29)
Ordering in a restaurant, pp.48–49
I booked a table for 8:30. The name's Millar.

What are the specials?
What's in a Greek salad?
Does it contain meat?
I can't eat nuts.

To start, I'll have the smoked salmon.
We'll have a bottle of the house red, please.
And a large bottle of water.
Do you have decaffeinated coffee?
Two coffees, please – one decaf.
Could we have the check, please?

Unit 8
(Track 30)
In my free time, pp.50–51
What do you do in your free time?
I go out with friends.
I go for a bike ride.

I play the guitar.
I play the drums.
I go dancing.
I go shopping.
I play football.
I play badminton.

(Track 31)
Talking about what I like, pp.52–53
I love
I really like
I like
I don't mind
I don't like
I don't like . . . at all
I hate

What do you like watching on television?
What kind of movie is it?
What do you want to watch tonight?
What's on?
When's the game show on?
My favorite movie is on tonight.
It's really exciting.
It's very informative and entertaining.
Documentaries are really boring.

I don't really like movies like that!
I sometimes watch dramas – if they're entertaining.
Not football again! It's always on!
That sounds really boring!
I prefer dramas to documentaries.

I don't mind watching the news.

(Track 33)
What I like doing, pp.54–55
When it's raining, I like watching DVDs.
When it's sunny, we like going for a walk in the country.
When it's snowing, I like staying in and reading books and magazines.
I go shopping in any weather!

What will we do tomorrow?
If it's warm tomorrow, we'll go swimming.
If it's hot on the weekend, I'll go to the beach!
If it's windy, we'll go for a walk.
If I have time this evening, I'll surf the internet.

If it's cold on Friday, I won't play tennis.

Unit 9
(Track 35)
I don't feel well, pp.58–59
How do you feel?
I don't feel well.

I have a sore shoulder.
I have a stomach ache.
My back is sore.
My throat is very sore.

My ear hurts.
My knee hurts.
My feet hurt.
My teeth hurt.

I have a cold.
I have a fever.
I feel achy.
I feel sick.
I feel dizzy.
I'm nauseated.

(Track 36)
At the pharmacy, pp.60–61
My head hurts.
I feel very tired.
My throat is sore too.
For four days.
Could you recommend something for a cold, please?
Do you have something for the flu?
Do you have something for insect bites?
It's for my husband.
He was bitten on the hand.
It's swollen.
It's really itchy.

I'll take the syrup, please.
Could I have some aspirin, please?
Could I have some cough syrup, please?
Could I have some Band-Aids, please?

(Track 38)
At the doctor, p.62–63
I'd like to make an appointment, please.
Can I make an appointment for my daughter, please?
For today, if possible.
For Tuesday.
Do you have anything on

Friday?
That would be fine.

I have a very sore throat.
My neck is also very stiff.
I feel tired all the time.
How often do I need to take the pills?

Unit 10
(Track 40)
Finding out about a job, pp.64–65
My name's . . .
I'm calling about your ad for language instructors . . .
. . . in Monday's paper.
Can you tell me more about the job?
That sounds very interesting.

I don't have experience as . . .
I can speak German.
I can speak some French.
I used to study piano.
I have experience working with children.
I really enjoy music.

(Track 41)
Applying for a job, pp.66–67
I grew up in Germany.
I studied education and music.
I took French classes as well.
I have experience in planning lessons.
I was in charge of summer school.
I had five teachers working for me.
I am looking for a job that will allow me to use my language skills.

Did you send off your application last week?
Yes, I did.
No, I didn't.
What did you say in your letter?

I said that I was interested in using my teaching degree.
I said I used to study music.

(Track 42)
At an interview, pp.68–69
I have a degree in marketing.
I have a degree in law.
I have a degree in psychology.

I'm fluent in German.
My Spanish is good.
I work well as part of a team.
I'm good at meeting deadlines.
I'm good with customers.
I have a clean driving record.
I managed the store when my boss was away.
I enjoy working with the public.
I would like the opportunity to develop my management skills.

I love traveling.
I would like the opportunity to use my German.
I enjoy working with young people and I'm good at it.
I studied it at college.
I lived in New York for a year as part of my course.
I didn't have any problems.
I enjoyed studying piano.
It didn't give me much opportunity to work with children.
I decided it was time to change.

Unit 11

(Track 44)
Returning something, pp.70–71
There's a problem with this necklace.
There's a problem with these shoes.
It's faulty.
It isn't working.
It's broken.
There's a mark.
There's a hole.
It's too small.
It's too big.
A piece is missing.
A button is missing.

I'd like to return this.
Here's the receipt.
I got it as a present.
I don't have the receipt.
I bought it here a few months ago.
I bought them in your Eastside store last week.

Could I exchange it?
Could I have a refund?
Could I have a store credit?

(Track 46)
Reporting a loss, pp.72–73
I've lost my suitcase.
I've lost my wallet.
I've lost my backpack.
My handbag has been stolen.
My purse has been stolen.

It's got my money, my credit cards and my driver's license in it.
It's got my passport, plane ticket and traveler's checks in it.
It's got my keys and my cell phone in it.

It's a red leather backpack – quite small.
It's a big blue suitcase.
I had it when I got on the train.
I might have left it by the newspaper kiosk.
I definitely didn't have it when I went to pay.

(Track 47)
Solving other problems, pp.74–75
I booked a ticket to Las Vegas on the 11:20 bus . . .
. . . but I was held up and I missed it.
Can I change the ticket?
When is the next bus?
If I could have a ticket for that one, please.
Do I have to pay again?

I've been waiting for an hour now.
My luggage still isn't here.
I came from Miami.
I changed flights in Atlanta.
I'm staying in a hotel here for two weeks.

Unit 12
(Track 48)
Sharing plans, pp.76–77
in spring
in the spring
last spring
this summer
next autumn
during the winter

I'm working in Chicago for two weeks.
I'm hoping to go on vacation after that.
I'm thinking of going to Italy.
I might go to Mexico.
I might not stay at the same hotel as last time.
I don't want anything too expensive.

Are you going away this summer?
Where are you going?
What about you?
Who with?
When are you going?
Where are you staying?

When would you go?
Where would you stay?

(Track 49)
Future intentions, pp.78–79
When I finish my degree, I'm going to work abroad.
When I leave school, I'll take a year off.
Before I'm forty, I'll be a millionaire.
After my children finish school, I'm going to do volunteer work in Africa.
In five years I want to open my own store.
This time next year I want to be head of Sales.

If I'm successful, I'll be very rich.
If I have a baby, I'd like to work more flexibly.
If it doesn't work out, I'd like to go back to college.
If I don't get promoted, I want to start my own business.
If I don't get a new job, I'm going to go back to school.

I don't know what I want to do.

Wordlist

Aa

a, an
about
abroad
accountant
address
after
afternoon
again
along
always
am (*present* be)
American
and
animals
another
antibiotics
any
anything
apple
apple juice
appointment
are (*present* be)
arm
arrive (to)
as far as
aspirin
at
aunt
Australia
Australian
autumn
available

Bb

back
backpack
badminton
bag
baker's
bandage
Band-Aids
bank
bank teller
banking

bar
baseball cap
be (to)
beer
before
beginner
belt
best
better
between
bike
black
blue
boarding pass
boat
book
book (to)
boots
boring
boss
bottle of wine
bottled water
bought (*past* buy)
box of chocolates
boyfriend
Brazil
Brazilian
breakfast
bridge
broken
brother
brown
budget
bus
bus station
bus stop
business
busy
by
Bye!

Cc

café
cake
call (to)

can
can't
car
carrots
carton
cartoon
catch (to)
CD
cell phone
change (to)
cheap
check
check in (to)
cheek
cheese
cheesecake
chef
chest
chicken
child / children
chin
China
Chinese
chips
chocolate
chocolates
city hall
class
coach
coat
coffee
cold
cold (a)
come (to)
comedy
commercial
company
computer
cook (to)
cookies
corner
cost (to)
cough syrup
country
cousin
credit card

crepe
cross (to)
cup
currently
customer
cute

Dd

dad / daddy
dance (to)
dancing
daughter
deadline
decaff(einated)
degree
delicious
dessert
did (*past* do)
direct
divorced
dizzy
do
do (to)
doctor
documentary
dollars
down
drama
dress
drink
drink (to)
driver's license
drums
due
DVD

Ee

ear
eat (to)
education
eggs
Egypt
Egyptian
elbow

e-mail
engineering
England
English
enjoy (to)
entertaining
evening
every
everything
exchange (to)
exciting
excuse me
expensive
experience
eye

Ff

family
far
father
faulty
favorite
fever
film
finance
fine
finger
finish (to)
fish
fit (to)
flight
flu
fluent
foot/feet
football
form
France
free
French
friend
from
fruit salad
fully booked
funny

Gg

game show
gave (*past* give)
German
Germany
get out (to)
get to (to)
girlfriend
glass
go (to)
golf
good
Good afternoon.
Good evening.
Good idea!
Good morning.
Good night.
grade school
grandparents
grapes
great
green
green salad
grey
grocery store
guitar
gym shoes

Hh

had (*past* have)
hair
ham
handbag
has (*present* have)
hat
hate (to)
have (to)
have to (to)
hayfever
he
head
headache
Hello.
help (to)
her
here
Here you are.
hers

Hi.
high school
his
history
hole
hospital
hot
hotel
hour
how
How are you?
how long?
how much/many?
hungry
hurt (to)

Ii

I
I'd like . . .
I'm sorry.
ibuprofen
ice-cream
identity card (ID)
if
ill
in
included
India
Indian
infection
informative
interested in
interesting
intersection
interview
is (*present* be)
it
Italian
Italy

Jj

jacket
Japan
Japanese
jeans
job
journalist

Kk

keys
knee
know (to)

Ll

lamb
language
large
last name
later
law
leave (to)
(on the) left
leg
letter
lettuce
level
library
like (to)
line (underground)
lips
live (to)
look (to)
look after (to)
lots of/a lot of
love (to)
lovely
luggage

Mm

main course
mark
market
marketing
married
math
maybe
meat
meet (to)
mend (to)
menu
milk
mine
minute

missing
mom/mommy
money
moped
more
morning
mother
motorcycle
mouth
movie theater
movies
moving
museum
mushroom
music program
musician
mussels
my
My name's . . .

Nn

name
near
neck
necklace
need (to)
never
new
news
newspaper
next (to)
night
night club
no
noisy
nose
not so good
now
number
nurse
nuts

Oo

of
of course
off-peak
OK

olives
on
on foot
on my/your own
on vacation
onions
opposite
or
orange
orange juice
organize (to)
ounces
over
over there
own

Pp

packet
pants
park
parking lot
passport
paté
pay (to)
peanuts
people
peppers
pharmacy
phone (to)
phone number
photo
photographer
piano
pills
pink
pint
pizza
place
plane
plane ticket
platform
play (to)
please
Pleased to meet you.
police officer
politics
post office
potatoes

pound
prescription
present
pretty
probably
problem
psychology
publishing
purple
purse

Qq

quite

Rr

radio
really
receipt
receptionist
recreation center
red
restaurant
restrooms
résumé
retired
return
return (to)
rice
(on the) right
risotto
road
room
Russia
Russian

Ss

sad
said (past say)
salad
salmon
same
sandals
sandwich
say (to)
scary
school

season
see (to)
See you soon.
sell
she
shirt
shoes
shop
shopping
shopping mall
shorts
shoulder
shower
sick
side order
sign (to)
since
sing (to)
single
sister
size
skills
skirt
small
so
soap
sociology
socks
some
sometimes
son
soon
sore
soup
south
Spain
Spanish
sparkling water
specials
spell (to)
spend (to)
spinach
sports program
spring
start (to)
stay (to)
steak
still
stomach

stop
stores
straight
strawberries
streetcar
strong
student
study (to)
subway
subway station
sugar
suit (to)
suitcase
suite
summer
supplement
sweater
sweatshirt
swimming
swimming pool

Tt

take (to)
talk show
taught (*past* teach)
taxi
tea
teach
teacher
team
television
term
terrible
thank you (very much)
thanks
that

that's right
the
the public
the United States
them
then
there are . . .
there's . . .
these
they
think (to)
thirsty
this
those
throat
throat lozenges
thumb
ticket
tie
tights
timetable
tired
to
today
toe
tomato
tomatoes
tomorrow
tongue
tonight
too
took (*past* take)
tooth/teeth
tourist
tourist information office
toy
train

train station
travel (to)
traveler's cheques
try (to)
try . . . on (to)
T-shirt
tube of cream
tuna
turn (to)

Uu

uncle
unemployed
university
use (to)
useful
valid
vegetables
very
very well

Ww

waiter/waitress
wallet
want (to)
warm
was (*past* be)
watch
watch (to)
water
we
weather forecast
week
weekend
went (*past* go)
were (*past* be)

what
What time is it?
What's your name?
when
where
which
white
windy
wine list
winter
with
work (to)
worse
worst
Would you like . . . ?
wrist
write (to)
wrong

Yy

yellow
yes
yet
you
you're welcome
your
yours